ESOTERIC PRAGUE

CUBIST PRAGUE

OTHER BOOKS IN ENGLISH PUBLISHED BY EMINENT

ESOTERIC PRAGUE
by Jiří Kuchař

THE PRAGUE HOROLOGE
by Jakub Malina

CHARLES BRIDGE
by Jakub Malina

THE CZECH CORONATION JEWELS
by Jan Boněk & Tomáš Boněk

KARLSTEIN
by Jan Boněk

RUDOLF II AND HIS IMPERIAL PRAGUE
by Jan Boněk

JEWISH PRAGUE
by Jan Boněk

BAROQUE PRAGUE
by Jan Boněk

THE PRAGUE CATHEDRAL
OF MATTHIAS OF ARRAS AND PETER PARLER
by Jan Boněk

PRAGA HERMETICA
by Martin Stejskal

More information at
www.eminent-books.eu

ESOTERIC PRAGUE

CUBIST PRAGUE

Four ingenious architects

The only Cubist café in the world

Little gems of houses

JAN BONĚK

EMINENT 2014

TABLE OF CONTENTS

ISBN 978-80-7281-469-5

CUBIST PRAGUE

It is a mystery which modern art experts have been trying to resolve for more than one hundred years. Why, at the beginning of the 20th century, did Prague and a few other Czech towns try to include **Cubism**, the last major avant-garde art movement, in architecture as well? Nothing like this happened anywhere else in Europe. It was only a short period of time, during which, however, almost 50 Cubist houses were built just in Prague alone in the years of 1909—1912 and again during 1918—1925 when architects were searching for a "national" architectural style in connection with the creation of independent Czechoslovakia. Many of them still exist and draw well-deserved attention. For instance, many admirers of Prague Cubist architecture from Germany, Italy, France and even Japan stop on a daily basis in the only Cubist café in the world, **Grand Café Orient** in the House of the Black Madonna (Prague 1 — Old Town, Celetná Street No. 34/569), according to the café's personnel.

It is seemingly not very complicated to understand how the phenomenon — Czech Cubism — was created. Shortly before the outbreak of WW I, the artworks of Prague artists belonged among the best that one could see at art exhibitions in Paris, Berlin, Brussels, Amsterdam and even in then hated Vienna. Next to the most renowned Czech painters, there was a third art center that, together with Paris and Ber-

Grand Café Orient, one of the most famous European cafés and perhaps one-of-a-kind in the world, was only open to the public during the years of 1912—1922. It was not reopened until the end of the 20th century.

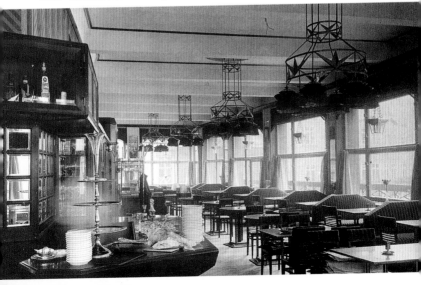

The French avant-garde paintings were presented in Prague before WW I at six exhibitions. "We, the young, were mostly interested in Braque," recalled Cubist painter, graphic artist and sculptor Emil Filla. This exhibition poster was made in 1907 by fine artist František Kysela.

lin, determined the development of modern European art. Even though it is still believed that Prague at the turn of the 19th and 20th centuries was just a dilapidated, grimy and overall backward "Cinderella" at the periphery of the Austro-Hungarian Empire, it is just not true. It is in Prague where a miracle happened during the first twenty years of the last century. In fact, one generation gave birth to many distinct artists who then created an independent art movement. Back then, the capital city was actually very open to everything modern. It was because every even slightly intelligent person understood that the empire was in trouble and would soon be finished. Politics stimulated art and vice versa.

Two shots fired from an old semi-automatic pistol Browning M 1910 by Latin Bridge on Sunday, 28 June 1914, at 10.45 a.m. changed history forever. The assassin shot Crown Prince of the Austro-Hungarian Empire Franz Ferdinand d'Este in the neck and his wife Sophia Chotek in the stomach. They both died.

Prague was the true center of Cubism before WW I and shortly after the foundation of Czechoslovakia. Young architects used Cubist axioms to design not only houses but also interiors. This picture from 1926 shows Josef Gočár's living room.

This promising trend was cut short by the gunshots in Sarajevo. The successful assassination of Crown Prince Ferdinand d'Este and his wife Sophia Chotek and the declaration of the war brought about hard times for art; however, the new lifestyle could no longer be stopped. Miroslav Lamač (1928—1992), a prominent Czech art historian and one of the most recognized experts on Czech fine arts of the beginning of the 20th century, once wittily said:

> *"From this point of view, Prague has become the true city of Cubism where Cubist houses were built and flats were filled with Cubist furniture. People could drink from Cubist coffee cups, put flowers in Cubist vases, use Cubist clocks to measure time and read books with Cubist lettering. The new art was to become (…) a distinctive form of modern esprit. Yet, Czech Cubism did not develop just from the ideas born in Montmartre; it is rooted in Expressionism and Art Nouveau while remaining tied to the national tradition of the Baroque and Gothic styles and following up on the spiritual heritage of the 19th century."*

However, Cubism did not just "drop from the sky." To understand the entire context and to appreciate the unique phenomenon of Prague — and partly also Czech — Cubist architecture, we must go back in European history.

THE ORIGINS OF CUBISM

It is said that Cubism was "discovered" around the year of 1906 by Spanish painter Pablo Picasso in his Parisian studio and by French painter George Braque in his studio in Barcelona, independently from each other. They started working together the following year and continued to do so until WW I. To some extent, this avant-garde movement was a result of the unsteady situation in France in the 19th century when Napoleon III decided to radically reconstruct Paris. The Parisians were against the reconstruction, but as prominent Czech architect Kamil Hilbert (1869 — 1933) says, it *"brought in fresh air and freed everyone's spirit."* It is because, except for some imposing palaces and cathedrals, Paris back then was as ugly as the Prague Jewish ghetto. The critics of the "spree of Baron Georges-Eugčne Haussmann in charge of transforming the city" often forget this fact, although the photographs from that era clearly prove it. With the new architectural concept, Paris took a deep breath toward a modern future, which also included new art movements.

At the turn of the century, young artists were also frustrated by the ornamental nature of ever-present Art Nouveau, which steered them toward surprising inspirational sources. Concurrently with art collectors, they became fascinated by African tribal masks, ancient Iberian sculptures and Micronesian and Native American art — a delightfully simple, abstract, direct and pure message. This art very much enthralled 26-year-old Pablo Picasso and gave him the key to express the complexity of his soul. His monumental oil painting *Les Demoiselles d' Avignon* [The Young Ladies of Avignon] of the dimensions 244 cm × 234 cm from 1907

In the fall of 1907, young painter Georges Braque, accompanied by poet Guillaume Apollinaire, entered for the first time Pablo Picasso's studio in Montmartre, which — to be more exact — was just a modest cellule of the young man with the reputation of a "child prodigy." It is believed that at first George Braque did not like Picasso's oil painting *The Young Ladies of Avignon* at all, but it soon influenced his artistic direction in a major way.

In the summer of 1908, Georges Braque made and exhibited in a small art gallery in Paris a series of paintings with the seaport town of L'Estaque, which marked the beginning of Cubist painting. A year later, he and Picasso grew together both humanly and artistically so much that only a real expert is able to tell which painting from that time period is whose.

is still considered his first Cubist artwork. He abandoned the palette of sugary colors of his earlier Blue and Rose Periods and surprised everyone with unusual, angular shapes. Shocked Parisians became disconcerted, and another round of criticism followed when it came to light that Picasso had not painted mondaines from papal Avignon but five nude prostitutes from the brothel at Avinyó Street in Barcelona. In fact, the painting was originally titled *The Brothel of Avignon*.

The year of 1908 was another important milestone. That year, 20-year-old Georges Braque exhibited several of his paintings depicting the seaport town of L'Estaque in a small Parisian art gallery owned by then unknown 24-year-old German art dealer Daniel Henry Kahnweiler. Renowned art critic Louis Vauxcelles made fun of these paintings in the daily Gil Blas, saying that they were full of **"bizarre cubiques"** (small bizarre cubes). And this is how the word Cubism was born, although it was meant pejoratively. The painters did not like this word and hoped that people would soon forget it, but it rather quickly caught on and with time lost its pejorative meaning.

So, how to define Cubism? In his first polemic with the critics of his artwork,

Georges Braque emphasized the need to bring excitement, to stir up emotions and to do away with the habit of imitating movement. According to him, it was mostly about capturing the three-dimensional reality limited by a two-dimensional canvas. He accentuated working with basic geometric shapes without the necessity to strictly observe the rules of perspective. The objective was to engage viewers through suspense, the mystery of form and an entirely new, open outlook of reality. What makes Cubism so interesting is its attempt to capture an object not just from one angle, but rather from different angles at the same time. It is about giving an artwork a proper space and using imagination that brings the deformed picture back to reality, even if it is very difficult to see the new relationships between the depicted objects. For the sake of completeness, let's just add that even for Cubist artists, it was not easy to comprehend the unrestrained metamorphoses of this art movement — from the exploration of a Cubist perspective to partial abstraction, where individual elements were no longer dependent on reality, all the way to a certain form of pure Cubism later on influenced by Surrealism. The use of colors changed as well — from plain gray and brown shades to all shades of color.

Cubism was immediately embraced by craftsmen as well, but it was more difficult for architects because Cubist buildings had to be functional as well. It took many years of searching for theoretical principles and choosing suitable construction materials, but in the end it all depended on stakeholders because it was always much more expensive to carry out Cubist projects. It is in fact a miracle that they were effectuated even if only during a short period of time and in one place in the world — in rich Prague and sporadically in Bohemia as well. Only in Prague did several architects manage to translate the vocabulary of Cubist compositions into the language of architecture. And what's more, they successfully incorporated the new edifices in the historical context of the city, in the whole variety of architectural styles defining the unique genius loci of Prague streets and squares.

THE STELLAR HOUR OF CZECH CUBISM

It is still believed that, except for a couple of decades during the reign of the Luxembourgs and the first Hapsburgs, Prague was just a sleepy provincial town unable to appreciate the great cultural heritage of past generations. It is not true. Since the reign of the first Premyslids, Prague has blossomed into a unique and literally pampered agglomeration of architectural styles creating its unparalleled atmosphere. Emperor and King Charles IV and Emperor Rudolf II understood the importance of investing in the residential city because this way they could amplify its beauty.

This was properly appreciated by Prague visitors even after many centuries had passed. Instead of mentioning dozens of prominent people who visited Prague, let's consider an excerpt from a letter dated 1902 written by otherwise very critical French sculptor Auguste Rodin and addressed to the Prague City Council: *"Prague is one of the most beautiful cities that I have ever seen. (…) It resembles Dante's Paradise."*

His exhibition in the Prague district of Smíchov was the height of the confrontation of Czech art with European art and presented the works of French, Russian, Polish, English, German and Austrian artists. Many of them have already fallen into oblivion, while others still shine like the brightest stars, such as Auguste Renoir, Edgar Degas, Claude Monet and Gustav Klimt. On the imaginary top is Norwegian painter Edvard Munch, who influenced the entire further development of Czech fine arts. A collective exhibition of his artwork, which took place in the Kinsky Garden in 1905, initiated the struggle for new art. It was endorsed not only by his contemporaries but also by future generations in spite of the fact that both townspeople and art critics unanimously rejected his artwork as the outcry of a lonely soul that has nothing in common with the suffering of modern day man.

It is understandable. Starting in the middle of the 19th century, fine arts had been infiltrated with so many ideas that it was often very difficult for conservative art lovers to understand the language of painters. This explains the literally hateful storm caused by eight young Prague painters

It is hard to believe nowadays that before WW I prominent modern painters from entire Europe regularly exhibited their artworks in Prague.

who were part of the group called The Eight. Influenced by Munch's exhibition, they displayed their paintings in 1907 and 1908. People were provoked just by their concept of color as an *"instrument of true mystical symbolism."* They were immature men with mature opinions, who sometimes despaired of being misunderstood. Their unofficial speaker Bohumil Kubišta voiced it the best in his letter from Paris to his friend Vincenc Beneš: *"We are too wild for Prague and too backward for Paris, we are suspended between the sky and the earth."*

They were not rightly appreciated until much later. Only time proved their quality. Their first exhibitions are now considered the onset of Czech modern art.

PARIS WITH THE ECHOING OF THE HOMELAND

One cannot talk about Cubist Prague without mentioning Paris. After all, six generations of artists drew their ideas and gained their experience in this most distinguished center of European art before they could say "now we have caught up." It is perhaps impossible to find a Czech painter, sculptor, writer or journalist who back then did not come to Paris even if just for a short period of time. These very young men, whose artistic career was just ahead of them, usually returned home but their heart remained in the city on the Seine. Painters Soběslav Pinkas and Jaroslav Čermák moved to Paris in the middle of the 19th century and were later on followed by painter Antonín Chittussi and writer Josef Václav Frič. Vojtěch Hynais, who painted the curtain of Prague's National Theatre, lived in Montmartre in 1878. However, the most accomplished was painter Václav Brožík, who became a member of the French Academy of Fine Arts and whose funeral in 1901 was attended by the mayor of Paris himself. Alfons Mucha stands apart, of course. He became famous literally overnight thanks to his poster Gismonda commis-

Antonín Chittussi (1847–1891), Václav Brožík (1851–1901), Vojtěch Hynais (1854–1925) and Josef Václav Frič (1829–1890).

Alfons Mucha in his Paris studio.

sioned by Parisian actress Sarah Bernhardt. He made many other posters for her that defined Parisian Art Nouveau for more than 20 years and that his admirers even took off posts.

And let's not forget poet, journalist and writer Jan Neruda, who — after his visit to the French metropolis at the beginning of the 1860s — returned completely enchanted by its radical transformation, for which Paris received 260 million Francs a year. Coincidentally, a couple of years later, the Prague City Council started discussing the redevelopment plan for dilapidated Josefov and some of the adjacent streets overreaching to the Prague Old Town. Influenced by his experience from Paris, Jan Neruda was one of the enthusiastic supporters of the redevelopment. Unfortunately, he overlooked some "tiny" details. The drastic demolition in Paris concerned slums, which had been built spontaneously around palaces and cathedrals and consisted of dark, narrow, crooked lanes with cheap houses without potable water and plumbing. Moreover, the project had an ulterior political motive. Emperor Napoleon III wanted to get the revolutionaries out of downtown Paris: *"A total of 350,000 people will be moved to the outskirts of Paris. Twelve boulevards will be as wide as possible to make it more difficult to build barricades and easier to redeploy the army."* Seventeen years later, the unfinished project was suspended.

It is true, Prague was infatuated with modernization and did not know when to stop. The passed redevelopment bills concerned not only Josefov but also a part of the Old Town and the New Town. The original list of 260 expropriated houses to be leveled to the ground was expanded to 624 houses. In their book *Dějiny Prahy* [History of Prague] (2000), Václav Ledvinka and Jiří Pešek say: *"… the then cursed redevelopment of the Jewish Town was actually nothing compared to the hurricane of private demolitions that swept through Prague in the last third of the 19th century and practically destroyed all Gothic, Renaissance and Baroque houses and palaces in the heart of the New Town as well as some parts of the Old Town and the Lessor Town."*

The large-scale modernization of Paris in the second half of the 19th century had its enthusiastic supporters as well as staunch opponents. Old pictures of the downtown of this ancient city on the Seine, which was as ugly as Prague's Jewish ghetto, prove the still-disputed reason for this extensive redevelopment.

Today, it has been proven beyond any doubt that before the "grand redevelopment paid for by the state," people were demolishing houses in Prague left and right without any permit and with minimum risk. Their motive was quite obvious: to outrun the law and to acquire expensive ground-plots with impunity.

Even though the modernization of other European cities, such as Vienna or Munich, was not spared of problems and fervent discussions, nowhere else were there so many contradicting opinions about the future architectural concept of a city as in Prague. Yet, it was not just about the concept of the new development but mostly about its incorporation in the historical context of the city. In heated disputes, people often talked about a decline of the nation, chaos-causing technocrats, cultural primitiveness and vandalism and the destruction of national taste and culture in general. Fortunately, many projects did not materialize. For instance, the Parisian-type boulevard, which was to start at the National Museum, cross the Old Town Square, where the Kinsky Palace would be sacrificed, go under Letná Hill and end in Dejvice, was not built only thanks to financial reasons. The construction project of a group of high-rises on Kampa Island and a riverbank road from Smíchov to Holešovice also failed, and so did the construction project of a direct four-lane road between Pohořelec and the Lessor Town Square (going through today's Neruda Street).

The changes in Prague's architecture at the turn of the 19th and 20th centuries were brutal, and many valuable buildings were destroyed. However, looking back, we can say that Prague preserved its historical look and, on top of it, more or less successfully incorporated Neo-Renaissance, Neo-Baroque and above all Art Nouveau edifices as well as the historical style featured mostly by architect Josef Zítek. The projects of Jan Kotěra, a pupil of Viennese architect Otto Wagner, and his successor Otakar Novotný completed the development of Prague architecture of the 19th century. Soon after came a style that perceived matter and spiritual elements in a different way and was directly influenced by the young generation of painters, sculptors, stage designers and writers. Prague was the only European city where these artists were joined by a group of architects. It is surprising, but the city was very much ready to embrace the new artistic style — Cubism.

Yes, surprising because one would think that such a polymorphic living organism would have encased itself in the past and would not have been able to absorb such a dramatic transformation. However, the

Unlike Paris, Prague constituted a magnificent architectural entirety, with the exception of the uncontrollably growing Jewish Town. All the more dangerous were the plans to build wide boulevards in Prague's historical center. They could have given the city a lethal blow. A good example is the "blind" Pařížská Street that was to start at the National Museum. For different reasons it was built only up to the hillside below the Prague district of Letná.

When visiting Prague in 1902, Guillaume Apollinaire, the most distinct figure of modern art, experienced something very unusual — one could even say something mystically symbolic. He actually saw his face in one of the agates in the St. Wenceslas Chapel of the Cathedral of St. Vitus. Josef Čapek later on made his portrait in a wood block. It was an incredible coincidence. Today, in spite of knowing what we are looking for, it is hard to find this agate on the facing of the chapel.

cultural history of Prague proves the remarkable ability of this city to embrace even very contrasting styles. This is what Guillaume Apollinaire appreciated already in 1902. Emotionally disturbed (perhaps also because of his strange experience in the Cathedral of St. Vitus where he saw his face in one of the agates in the St. Wenceslas Chapel and supposedly fainted and was not quite himself for several days), this French poet and playwright and one of the most prominent admirers and promoters of Cubism realized the power of such an ancient culture, which he at first noticed only through the present. He may have been the first person to understand that Prague was literally "impregnated with a creative revolution."

He had only expressed what young architects in Prague felt several years later. According to many published testimonials, they quite intentionally and feverishly searched for bygone values, knowing that they were somewhat lost in time. Well, this too was part of that era. The new art devoured them. They realized that it was a universal style that could be used not only in painting, but also in sculpture, applied arts and architecture. Someone once said that a hundred articles and essays had been written to defend the use of this revolutionary art movement in architecture before the first Cubist edifice had even been built. For these architects, Cubism was the acme. However, contrary to architects in other countries, they believed in old great European art eras and admired the Romanesque, Gothic and Baroque styles. Let's mention a few examples... Before the year of 1910, perhaps all talented and promising thirty-year-old artists, such as Emil Filla, Otto Gutfreund, Otakar Kubín, Bohumil Kubišta, Antonín Procházka, Josef Čapek and later on also Jan Zrzavý, visited France. Some of them were lucky enough to see the studios of Cubist painters thanks to Vincenc Kramář, an art historian and a great expert in everything new that France embraced. In the Louvre, they examined the rules of composition and the way of working with colors, which was impossible to do on black and white reproductions back home.

Later on, they talked about their experience and observations in *Umělecký měsíčník* [Art Monthly], the magazine of the Group of Fine Artists (published only during 1911—1913 due to financial reasons). Its editor, Josef Čapek, called it "the loud-hailer" of Czech Cubists. Full of admiration, they wrote about their inspiration by medieval artworks that they had seen e.g. in the Vézelay Abbey — the Basilica of St. Mary

---

Vincenc Kramář (1877—1960), a Czech art theoretician and recognized European historian, majorly contributed to the understanding of the artistic value of Cubism. Although misunderstood for many years, he became famous as a foresighted collector. His collection of French Cubist paintings is considered one of the best in the world. This wedding picture from 1912 shows Vincenc Kramář with his new wife Marie Goldnagl, born to a prominent Viennese family.

Magdalene, which houses great Romanesque paintings. They had seen wonderful artworks in the Cathedral of St. Lazarus from the 12th century in Autun, Burgundy, and in the Moissac Abbey of the Benedictines with the most prominent monastery in the northeast of France. Its tympanum on the south portico is one of the European medieval masterpieces. They enthusiastically spoke of the Czech Baroque style that corresponded with Cubist aesthetics, the Empire style, the Classicist style and the art of the end of the 19th century. In brief, they found inspiration anywhere they looked.

Czech Cubist artists looked for inspiration for instance in France — in the Basilica of St. Mary Magdalene of the Vézelay Abbey, which houses great Romanesque paintings, in the Cathedral of St. Lazarus from the 12th century in Autun, Burgundy, and in the Moissac Abbey of the Benedictines with the most prominent monastery in the northeast of France. Its tympanum on the south portico is one of the European medieval masterpieces.

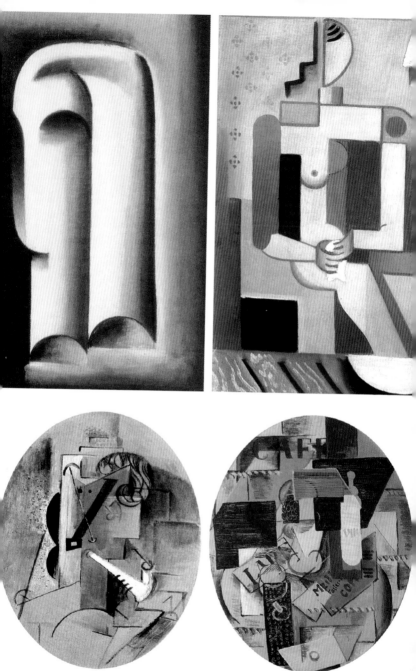

Cubist paintings of Czech artists are the centerpiece of many art galleries. Some Czech painters became famous not only in Europe but also around the world. For instance, the artworks of Emil Filla, Otakar Kubín, Václav Špála and Otto Gutfreund are always the pride of art auctions.

The Academy of Fine Arts in Vienna is one of the most notable and oldest art universities in Europe. It has raised many prominent artists since its foundation at the end of the 17th century. In the late 1800s, many talented students of architecture decided to study there because of professor Otto Wagner, whose book *Moderne Architektur* (Modern Architecture) from 1895 influenced the thinking and artwork of several generations of young artists, including Czech ones.

PRAGUE CUBIST ARCHITECTURE

We have discussed the creation of the unique artistic style and its penetration into our country only in general. The peculiar phenomenon — Czech Cubism — has been forever embedded in art history, mostly thanks to architecture. Coincidentally, there were several exceptional architects in Prague who developed this topic theoretically before the construction started. The implementation of their projects was faced with many problems, but luckily they found some stakeholders willing to take a financial risk. There is a simple answer to why architects did not emerge concurrently with painters right after Cubism was created: most of them were still in school at the beginning of the 20th century and, let's admit it, they were still grasping and searching for the philosophical framework of their plans.

Pavel Janák (1882—1956), who formulated the fundamental aspects of Cubism, became their leader. He was born in the Prague district of

Karlín as the middle son of a real estate broker and obtained his secondary education at a Czech grammar school in Ječná Street, Prague 2. Later on, he described himself as a quiet student unable to speak in front of a big group of people and an enthusiastic observer able to only write down and comment on other people's ideas. Against the will of his parents, Janák started studying structural engineering and architecture at the Czech Technical University under professor Josef Schulz, a renowned representative of Romanticism and Historicism who reconstructed e.g. the burned down National Theatre and built such magnificent edifices as Rudolfinum, the Museum of Decorative Arts and the National Museum.

Apparently dissatisfied with both the school and his teacher, Pavel Janák transferred to the German Technical University two years later and most likely picked the class of professor Josef Zítek, the most prominent Czech architect of the 19th century who represented the Czech Neo-Renaissance style and built e.g. the National Theatre in Prague and the Mill Colonnade in Carlsbad. This obviously still was not enough for Pavel Janák and so he signed up for Jan Kotěra's lectures in the special class of decorative architecture at the Academy of Arts, Architecture and Design. This is where he learned about the modern style

Janák's teacher Josef Schulz built such magnificent edifices as Rudolfinum and reconstructed the burned down National Theatre.

and literally gushed over it. He may have realized his lack of experience and therefore in 1904 interrupted his studies and began working as a designer for several Prague architects. Two years later, feeling that he had learned enough and had a sufficient amount of money in his bank account, Pavel Janák registered at the Academy of Fine Arts in Vienna. Although his dream to study under famous Otto Wagner came true, he only stayed there for two semesters. Even so, his teacher was very impressed by him and in July 1909 wrote the following about Pavel Janák's talent:

> *"You filled me with the most exhilarating hopes during the short period of time you were in my class."*

Pavel Janák left because he had received a very good scholarship of 1,615 Crowns a year from the Travel Fund for Czech Architects and Engineers bequeathed by architect Alois Turek (1810 —1893). The scholarship required him to study in Rome and to write a detailed paper so that he would learn about European architecture. Thus he traveled around Italy, France, Belgium, the Netherlands and Germany.

Almost immediately after his return to Prague in the fall of 1907, he was offered to work in Jan Kotěra's studio. Finally, he was in the middle of the action and among "his kind of people." Their teamwork led to the construction of pavilions for the Jubilee Exhibition in 1908, but this is also where it ended since Pavel Janák pined for his own independent projects. In 1909, he was hired as an architect of the Bridge Department of the Prague Construction Office and was assigned his first major proj-

A rare picture from Jan Kotěra's studio taken in 1907. The first person on the left is Pavel Janák.

Pavel Janák's dream about Cubist architecture was born with extreme difficulties. He needed to transform his theory into practice and so he had a lot of work to do. For instance, in 1909 he made a design for the addition of the Old Town Hall and for the completion of the Bridge of Hlávka.

ect — the Bridge of Hlávka joining the Prague districts of Holešovice and Těšnov. This first concrete bridge in Prague became the landmark of his work because it was not only functional but also had a dynamic feel to it. In his own opinion, he thus relinquished the exaggerated rationality of Jan Kotěra — the "father of modern Czech architecture" — which for him lacked emotional elements. Pavel Janák, Kotěra's enthusiastic follower turned critic, claimed that *"the material and structure determined too much the character of buildings."*

He presented this principal idea in his article *Od moderní architektury k architektuře* [From Modern Architecture to Architecture] in the magazine Style in 1910. For him, the Neo-Classicist, Neo-Gothic and Neo-Baroque styles were outdated since they did not deal with the basic aspects of space, material and form. He was fascinated e.g. by the prism that he analyzed in detail in the mineralogical collections of the National Museum. Pavel Janák *"rejects the simple form of the prism that only gives the impression of zero tranquility and prefers diagonal lines evoking dramatic feelings, directional movement and sharpness."*

In a somewhat complicated way, he compared Antique and Christian architecture, concluding that the biggest difference between static

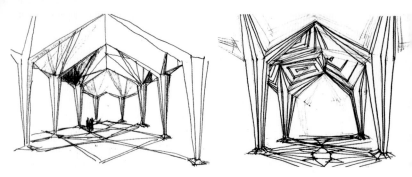

Pavel Janák's ideas about Cubist architecture often lacked a realistic basis. He overlooked structural possibilities, but was full of imagination.

Antique columns and beams and Gothic pillars and vaults rests in the energy of used materials. The Gothic style apparently inspired him the most in formulating his theory of Cubist architecture. During the years of 1911 — 1914, he published a great number of articles and comprehensive essays on this topic. Without them, Prague Cubist architecture would probably not exist. In truth, only several architects of similar visions, education and age embraced his revolutionary ideas, as the absolute majority of his colleagues dismissed them. Many architects had not yet relinquished the outdated, but still popular, Historicism of the 19th century, while others still worshipped already obsolete Art Nouveau or perhaps the Modernism of Jan Kotěra.

Janák's dream about what European architecture should look like did not come true. In the end, even he was disappointed by Cubism and, embittered, abandoned it in 1913. After WW I, he tended toward art movements promoting the "national style," also called Rondocubism or Czech Art Deco. He found his own way and, in addition to public functional buildings, designed "residential units" typical for their simplicity and colored details. He designed the Czechoslovak pavilion in the "national" style for the World Exhibition in Rio de Janeiro in 1922. But Prague was his love. He made many projects and designs for the urban concept of different Prague districts — Troja, Nusle, Holešovice, Podolí and Letná. He also renovated historical buildings, putting to use his lifelong interest in history; for instance, he helped to renovate the Černín Palace during the years of 1928—1934. In 1936, he was appointed the architect of the Prague Castle, replacing Josip Plečnik, and almost entirely focused on the reconstruction of historical edifices and the protection of Prague monuments.

Josef Gočár (1880—1945) is the second out of the four founders of Czech Cubist architecture. Although, he should have primacy since Josef

Gočár supposedly built everything Pavel Janák had invented. His Cubist and Rondocubist edifices are the best modern-style buildings ever built in our country. He was born to the family of a brewer in the little village of Semín by Přelouč. After his baccalaureate at a grammar school in Pardubice and short studies at the State Technical College, he was accepted to the Academy of Arts, Architecture and Design in 1902. At first, he studied in the atelier of Jan Kotěra as an ir-

regular student and then, thanks to his extraordinary talent, as a regular student in Jan Kotěra's school. After having completed his studies and returned from several foreign trips, he became the architect-in-chief of Kotěra's private studio before opening his own atelier. Josef Gočár fell in love with the new architectural style that had come to Prague. He made his first Cubist designs and obtained interesting commissions. With Pavel Janák, he founded the Group of Fine Artists and became its first chairman. Just for the sake of completeness, let's add that all architects mentioned in this book were members of this group and published the already mentioned *Art Monthly* where they publicized their articles on Cubism. However, Josef Gočár was not much into theorization. Except for reports accompanying his projects, he supposedly never wrote anything about Cubism and instead built the edifice that has become the pillar of Cubism — the House of the Black Madonna with the famous Grand Café Orient. His fascination with avant-garde did not last long either.

At his age of 44, he became a professor at the Academy of Fine Arts in Prague and moved his atelier from the Kotěra villa to the School of Architecture adjacent to the main building of the Academy of Fine Arts that Jan Kotěra had designed. He taught until the year of 1939, when Czech universities were closed down. He did not return to the academy after WW II ended due to his health problems and retired early. Josef Gočár, the most prominent Czech architect of the 20th century according to a survey from 2000, raised an entire generation of his successors who defined Czech architecture of the 1930s and partly also of the 1940s.

This lanky young man with black hair and piercing eyes confidently entered the world of architecture to become the leader of Prague culture. He was sought-after company in then popular cafés where he spent almost every afternoon. He always wore traditional English suits and smoked cigars like a true gentleman.

Vlastislav Hofman (1884—1964) is the third architect influenced by Cubism. He came from the family of a shoemaker in Jičín. After his baccalaureate at a grammar school, he tried to enter the Academy of Arts, Architecture and Design in Prague but failed and thus "settled for" structural engineering and architecture at the Czech Technical University where he studied under professor Josef Schulz.

He was a man of many professions: an architect, town planner, theoretician of Cubism and architecture, painter, graphic artist, designer and first and foremost a stage designer. People called him the Leonardo da Vinci of Czech avant-garde. Right after his graduation, he applied for the position of architect of the Construction Office in Prague and was hired. In this position, he greatly influenced the development of pre-war Prague and helped to save the Baroque ramparts around the Prague Castle. During the 41 years of his career in the Prague City Council, he designed e.g. the Bridge of Jirásek, the Bridge of Štefánik, Nusle Bridge and the footbridge for Jewish Island (today called Children's Island) in the Prague district of Smíchov.

He was only 25 years old when he designed furniture for Artěl, one of the most important institutions of Czech applied arts and design of the first half of the 20th century; this furniture is still considered an exceptional example of Cubism in applied arts. In spite of his young age, he rigorously implemented his vision that in Cubism *"angularity is right and its arbitrariness is preceded by excitement and a sudden idea."*

He sincerely professed this avant-garde form of art his entire life. Meeting Karel Hugo Hilar, director of the Municipal Theatre of Vinohrady, was the breaking point of his career. The two modern-minded artists understood each other so well that, at the age of 35, Vlastislav Hofman was given his first commission as a stage designer. He became rather quickly famous in this field and, during his lifetime, created

more than 400 stage designs for the Municipal Theatre of Vinohrady as well as for the National Theatre in Prague and the Municipal Theatre of Brno. He also designed costumes and masks. In 1924, he even received the Czechoslovak State Prize for Stage Designing thanks to his gift for artistically expressing his ideas with minimum means, which was true about everything he made.

Josef Chochol (1880—1956) is the last of the four representatives of Czech Cubist architecture. This native from Písek studied at the Czech Technical University for six years and at the Academy of Fine Arts in Vienna, under professor Otto Wagner, for three years. Shortly after, he abandoned the style of Viennese Art Nouveau to become one of the most admired architects of Prague Cubism. He welcomed the new art movement mostly because, in his opinion, contemporary art lacked *"emotionality, imagination and excitement."*

Before WW I, he built two apartment buildings and one family house, which brought fame both to him and to Cubist architecture in general. Thanks to Josef Chochol, Cubist architecture became one of those immortal experiments forever ingrained in history. The photographs of these buildings are rightfully included in the brochures of travel agencies around the entire world.

Later on, we will also mention other architects who gave the world absolutely unique Cubist architecture. It was a very peculiar style expressing the esoteric aspect of life. Enthralled, we ask in vain why such a brilliant exclamation of modern architects did not find any successor. It was perhaps because back then they all were too young and unchained and purposely ignored obstacles. Brick walls had to be cut and the use of concrete in construction was just at its beginnings, which very much slowed down the construction works and significantly raised the cost of construction projects.

Yet, their buildings are sheer architectural miracles. But how to arrange them? By architects? One would have to run around entire Prague and the overall impression would be lost anyway. To arrange them by the date of their construction is not a good solution either. Prague Cubist architecture was born in two stages and during a very short period of time, so even renowned experts could not figure out exactly when the construction of each building had started and finished. Therefore, it seems the best to map Cubist buildings by location. After all, there are not so many places as to totally exhaust those who are ready for some exciting moments.

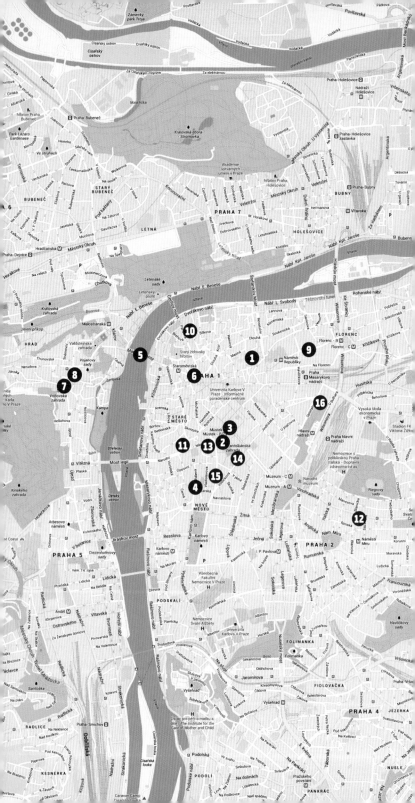

Inner Prague

1 The House of the Black Madonna
(also called the House of the Golden Grille)

Prague 1–Old Town
Celetná Street 34/569, Fruit Market 19

It is the most noted Cubist edifice of Prague and probably also of Europe, although the purity of its architectural style is sometimes disputed. In 1910, fabric wholesaler František Josef Herbst commissioned **Josef Gočár** to build him a department store perhaps because of the earlier success of this 31-year-old architect with the Wenke department store in Jaroměř and with the villa of Karel Jarušek, administration director of Lidové noviny, in Brno–Královo Pole. The prestigious building on the old Royal Route was a challenge in itself and the stakeholder's extremely complicated requests made it even more difficult. This may also be why he hired a young man having no "experience" with endless dealings with the Prague City Council and the then powerful Society for the Protection of Old Prague. The officials set down uncompromising conditions that rather limited the architect's creativity. The basic requirement was that *"the size and overall concept of the new building would not interfere in any way with the historical surroundings."* Gradually, more requirements were added, such as *"the façade must be in the modern style, expressing contemporary architectural ideas and satisfying modern needs."*

The new edifice was to replace two Late-Baroque houses and was named after the little statue of the Black Virgin Mary behind a golden grille, which used to be on one of these houses. The house was owned by the Knights of Granov, incredibly wealthy collectors of custom duty in nearby Ungelt where all foreign merchants coming to Prague had to stop. Josef Gočár very quickly submitted the first version of his architectural design and the proceedings started already in the middle of 1911. The critical analysis was prepared by conservator Dr. Luboš Jeřábek, the leader of the conservative wing of the Society for the Protection of Old Prague, the author of several books on the historical appearance of Prague and the terror of all architects. The Prague City Council accepted such a distinguished person's objections — the windows are too big, the cornice is robust, the columns between the windows are too angular, the roof is not inclined enough and the Virgin Mary statue is too high — without any reservation.

Most likely, Dr. Luboš Jeřábek wanted to discourage the young architect. Josef Gočár not only did not give up and redid his design within a couple of months, but also surprisingly added more Cubist elements, such as the angular face wall and windows, the multi-level mansard roof and the Cubist entrance and balcony railing. This version of his design was approved rather quickly supposedly because a group of young architects and urban development theoreticians with modern opinions on the protection of historical monuments had taken over the management of the Society for the Protection of Old Prague. The construction began immediately and, on 25 July 1912, the first key Cubist edifice in Prague was given the final building approval.

Josef Gočár designed the house on a pentagonal ground-plan and divided its angular face wall with simple cornices between the floors and the balcony. He placed the statue of the Black Madonna with the Infant Jesus right above the cornice of the store downstairs. The house was built with a reinforced concrete skeleton that allowed for a large interior space. The basement originally housed a wine bar and on the ground floor was the renowned store with fabrics, clothing and fashion goods. The floor above was made into the only Cubist café in the world, called Grand Café Orient, with sturdy black furniture and Cubist wallpaper and chandeliers designed by Josef Gočár as well. On the remaining floors were offices and the administrator's studio apartment and office and in the attic was a wash-house. The individual floors were connected with a staircase with Cubist adornment.

This original edifice of Josef Gočár in such a mystic location very much charmed Czech poet Jaroslav Seifert, who mentioned it in his poem *Modlitba na chodníku* [Prayer on the Sidewalk] included in his collection of poems called *Město v slzách* [City in Tears] (1921). Here is a little excerpt:

Pensive
I reached the corner of Fruit Market and Celetná
and kneeling down on the sidewalk,
I raised my eyes to the black Madonna,
who is standing here
and over my head she holds her hand,
and I prayed:
Virgin Mary, since it is necessary that I too die,
don't let me die like that dog (…)

The House of the Black Madonna is ingenious in many different respects. Its architect, Josef Gočár, tastefully dealt with the requests of the stakeholder, wholesaler František Herbst, as well as with the many requirements of the Prague City Council. He evidently realized the historical value of the space almost in the middle of Prague's Old Town that he had at his disposal.

The House of the Black Madonna was very well received, considering the time and the location. It was discussed in tabloids and architecture magazines as well as in the prestigious magazine Der Architekt in Vienna. In short, Josef Gočár had created a masterpiece that changed his life. He became a sought-after architect, new commissions were pouring in and he forever made his mark in the history of architecture.

After WW I, the café and the store were transformed into a bank and after 1948, the house was taken over by the state exhibition agency called Výstavnictví. The house was completely reconstructed and returned to its original state in the early 1990s.

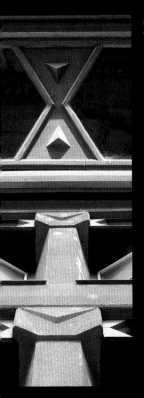

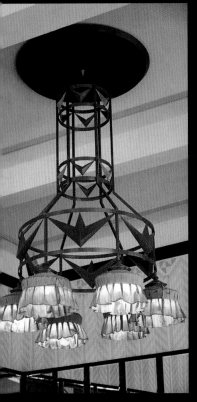

2 The Mozarteum

Prague 1–New Town
Jungmannova Street 30/748

Jan Kotěra (1871–1923)

It seems that the Mozarteum designed by **Jan Kotěra**, the most prominent representative of Czech modern architecture, should not even be in this book about Czech Cubism. It was built during the years of 1912—1913, which means about the same time when the House of the Black Madonna, the most famous building of his pupil Josef Gočár, was finished. At that time, there probably was an undeclared, yet all the more obvious, battle between geometric Modernism enthusiasts and the promoters of Cubism. While Jan Kotěra was never tempted by the rather original Cubist concept, it took his younger peers and pupils several years to discover that Cubist architecture may be interesting, but does not provide any possibility for further development.

Although Jan Kotěra was never considered a Cubist architect, we may perhaps dare to say that without him, this architectural style would not exist. He was born in Brno in 1871 as the younger son of a drawing teacher. After his baccalaureate at the school of civil engineering in Pilsen, Jan Kotěra worked as an intern in the designing office of Ing. Freyn, who also received commissions from Baron Mladota of Solopysky. They both recognized the young man's exceptional talent and paid for his further studies at the Academy of Fine Arts in Vienna under professor Otto Wagner, who had just been hired. Jan Kotěra proved to be an excellent student and, at the age of 26, was awarded the prestigious Rome Prize for his design of a tunnel under the English Channel, which included a grant at Palazzo Venezia in Rome and allowed him to travel around Italy in 1898. After his return, he was offered to teach in the special school of decorative architecture at the Academy of Arts, Architecture and Design in Prague and was expected to bring a fresh breeze to the local staleness.

Unfortunately, his first architectural project — Peterka's House (Prague 1, Wenceslas Square 12/777) — did not meet the exorbitant expectations. "The savior of Czech architecture" was right to suspect

After his arrival to Prague, Jan Kotěra somewhat naively tried to "save Czech architecture." He came up against a brick wall. His first building, Peterka's House at Wenceslas Square, became the target of practically personal attacks by conservative critics who were joined by the general public.

The Mozarteum in Jungmannova Street is wrongly considered a typical example of Classical Cubism because architect Jan Kotěra designed it in the modern architectural style and as an illustration of the "structural poetics" taught by Otto Wagner, his professor at the Academy of Fine Arts in Vienna. The building was finished in 1913 and later on paradoxically housed several exhibitions of Cubist painters.

that Vienna Art Nouveau would not fare well in Prague and so he opted for the Belgian-French version. But that did not work either. The conservatives unanimously decried the house, saying that he had brought *"to Prague distasteful fashion from hostile Vienna."* Everything that he believed in was discredited. His concept of eliminating all useless historical elements was not understood. In 1910, Jan Kotěra was appointed the professor of a new special school of architecture at the Academy of Fine Arts and yet had to wait almost 13 years for another major independent project.

He finally defended his architectural vision with the design of the Mozarteum department store built for music publisher Mojmír Urbánek. This austere building in the geometric modern style, which later entered the history of Czech culture, was very much unlike the other surrounding buildings because of its high oblong face wall crowned with a triangular gable. What also made the Mozarteum spectacular was its floor-by-floor receding façade. The building pillars at the street level were adorned with female statues made by the studio of Jan Štursa, while the façade of the upper, residential section was brick-faced.

Its reinforced concrete skeleton made it possible to open the ground floor toward the street and to connect it with a concert hall that could hold up to 400 people. The interesting thing is that the capitals of the bearing pillars are in the Cubist style; it may be that someone inconspicuously passed them to Jan Kotěra. The concert hall opened with Ema Destinová's concert. This is also where Arthur Rubinstein and Edvard Grieg performed and Le Corbusier and Rudolf Steiner gave lectures.

In the 1930s, this concert hall with the best acoustics in Prague was reconstructed into a theatre and housed the avant-garde D34 Theatre with its first director Emil František Burian. In the first half of the 20th century, the Mozarteum was one of the most sought-after centers of Prague intellectual and artistic life. In 1948, the concert hall was remodeled into a recording studio of the Supraphon Company. After the year of 1991, the whole dilapidated building was returned to its original owners — the Urbánek family — and, after a long reconstruction, regained its original splendor.

3 The Streetlamp by Adam's Pharmacy

Prague 1–New Town
Wenceslas Square 8 /775, (from
the back) Jungmann Square 14

Built on a small piece of land during the years
of 1912—1913, Adam's Pharmacy at Wenceslas
Square was basically a residential building with
a medieval basement that still exists. It is a great
example of the combination of Late Art Nouveau
and Cubist elements.

Emil Králíček
(1877–1930)

Prestigious Prague builder Matěj Blecha hired
young talented draftsman **Emil Králíček** (1877—
1930), who had just finished working on the construction of the
Darmstadt Artists' Colony founded by the Grand Duke of Hesse. Emil
Králíček first designed Art Nouveau façades with floral ornaments for
his employer, later on became fascinated by geometry and Modernism, went through a short Cubist period but built his masterpiece
in the Art Deco style. Experts regard him as a phenomenal eclectic
who achieved wonderful details through different means of expression. Emil Králíček was promoted to the position of senior designer
and later on opened his own studio. In the end, he committed suicide
probably due to financial or family problems.

After having read Janák's article, *The Prism and the Pyramid*, in the
magazine *Art Monthly*, Emil Králíček became immediately intrigued
by remarkable, yet impractical, Cubist architecture. However, he was
not as radical as some of his peers and designed only Cubist objects
for his buildings, such as the stone decorative vases by the staircase
of Adam's Pharmacy.

An ostensible small thing — a streetlamp created from truncated
cones placed on top of each other and decorated only with alternat-
ing grooved and smooth triangles — became the icon of the unique

In close proximity to hated Peterka's House, Emil Králíček made Adam's
Pharmacy in the Late Art Nouveau style based on Jan Kotěra's design. It
probably would not have become part of the history of Prague Cubist
architecture if the Prague City Council had not ordered to revitalize the
neglected area behind the pharmacy.

The column and illuminator of the streetlamp at Jungmann Square became the symbol of Cubism. Unfortunately, its faithful copy now sticks right out of the pavement rather than the original grassy area that had to yield to the pedestrian zone.

Cubist style. The illuminant itself made of metal and glass is of Cubist shape as well. The streetlamp is there because when Adam's Pharmacy was designed, the Prague City Council ordered to revitalize the much neglected area behind the pharmacy leading to Jungmann Square. Therefore, in 1912, the damaged pavement and the garden wall with a portal behind the Church of Our Lady of the Snow were repaired and a valuable Gothic tympanum from 1347 was placed above the original gate, based on the design of Emil Králíček. Since this area was very dark, the architect decided to give it some intimate lighting. There is a drawing that shows not only the entire reconstruction of the area but also an onlooking bartender from the local Pinkas Pub.

The original streetlamp started to dilapidate and therefore was replaced with its faithful copy. Unfortunately, the little grassy areas with a brick border where the streetlamp originally stood had to give way to the pedestrian zone built at the beginning of the 1980s, and so one of the admired symbols of Prague Cubism sticks right out of the pavement. The repaired original of the streetlamp is kept in the collections of the Gallery of the Capital City of Prague.

4 The Diamond House

Several architects were interested in the construction project of this apartment building with street-level stores at the great location on the corner of Spálená Street and Lazarská Street at the turn of the 19th and 20th centuries. The design of Austrian architect Friedrich Ohmann, made in the Late Historicist style, won. However, the in-progress construction of the Diamond House was suspended perhaps in the middle of 1912 and the building was redesigned by **Emil Králíček**, architect of the Blecha construction company, in the Art Nouveau and Cubist styles. Its new owner Adolf Hoffmeister, an attorney, an enthusiastic promoter of everything new and the father of the famous writer, painter and accomplished diplomat of the same name, approved the final design and filed the final building approval request in September 1913. The new building caused a lot of uproar among historical monument conservators and the conservatives of the Society for the Protection of Old Prague, who were angry mostly because of the Cubist alcove around the statue of St. John of Nepomuk between the Diamond House and the Church of the Holy Trinity. The statue was originally in a Baroque alcove, which was moved to the garden and turned into a water fountain. Heated discussions concerning this "unapproved provocation" were finally put to rest with the start of the war. By the time the war was over, the flood of emotions had subsided.

The name "Diamond" is perfect for the building since Emil Králíček decorated its artificial stone façade with crystalline shapes — vases, windows and bays. The adornment was spiced up with a couple of figures in the Cubist style from sculptor Antonín Waigant (1880—1918), who was once a sought-after interior architect and made sculptures only occasionally for the construction projects of his friends. Today, hardly anybody knows him, contrary to his younger brother Bohumil Waigant, an accomplished architect of geometric Modernism.

The Diamond House has many other Cubist elements, such as the staircase railing, window glass and lamps. The entrance portal from Spálená Street in particular drew a lot of attention from the very beginning and was copied several times both in and outside of Prague.

The Diamond Palace represents perhaps an isolated attempt to employ Cubist principles in the interior as well. Emil Králíček designed polygonal corner rooms with doors running on a diagonal axis. Let's just add that the architect angered the activists of the Society for the Protection of Old Prague by placing the Cubist alcove around the statue of St. John of Nepomuk between the Diamond Palace and the Church of the Holy Trinity.

5 The Bridge of Mánes

Prague 1–Old Town
joining Jan Palach Square in the Old Town
and Klárov in the Lessor Town

The river crossing at the place of today's Bridge of Mánes was used by merchants already in the 10th century and was part of one of the most important trade routes in Europe, which started somewhere in the Kingdom of León on the Iberian Peninsula and ended in Cracow, maybe even farther. The first place to get safely across the Vltava River was between the Prague district of Klárov and the so-called Rejdiště in the Jewish Town. The original wooden footbridge was replaced with the so-called Rudolf Footbridge in 1868—1869, named after Crown Prince Rudolf, the son of Franz Joseph I and Empress Elizabeth of Bavaria nicknamed Sissi.

This suspension bridge, also called the Iron Footbridge or the Chain Footbridge, was used, without having undergone any major repair, until the year of 1912 when the construction of a stone bridge started. This location was complicated from the urbanistic viewpoint mainly because of the nearby skyline of the Prague Castle. The construction was overseen by the Bridge Department of the Construction Office of the Prague City Council, and the blueprints were signed by architect Mečislav Petrů, head of the Construction Office. In truth, Ing. Alois Nový and Ing. František Mencl, a famous architect who influenced the current look of Prague, considerably participated in the project. The blueprints were changed several times. In 1912, it was decided — most likely due to financial reasons — that the bridge with four arches would be made of reinforced concrete and stone would be used only on its face wall and cornices.

The sole authorship of architect Mečislav Petrů has been doubted for a long time also because architects Pavel Janák, Josef Hofman and Josef Chochol, who were enthusiastic promoters of Cubism and most likely out of work at that time, collaborated with the Construction Office. They were probably the ones to suggest that the sculptural adornment of the bridge celebrating the life of Vltava raftsmen be made by František Bílek (the middle pillar), Josef Mařatka (the adjacent pillars) and Jan Štursa (the end pillars with the reliefs of Beauty and Art). Unfortunately, we do not know who made the Cubist barrier with the street light columns.

The Bridge of Mánes was rightfully immortalized on Czechoslovak stamps. It is one of Prague's very interesting monuments because it is well-balanced and has many decorative details. After all, this was best guaranteed by the long list of famous artists who worked on the bridge. Let's just add that the bridge is 186 meters long and 16 meters wide.

But we do know who made the beautiful fountains on both sides of the right bridge-head that started spouting water on 22 June 1925. These angular, Cubist fountains formed an imaginary pyramid, and their shallow basins with decorative diamond-shaped elements were filled with water from spouts in the shape of a human head. This daring work of art, literally a stone symphony of Cubism, was made by sculptor Emanuel Halman (1873—1945), a pupil of famous sculptor Josef Václav Myslbek. Emanuel Halman and accomplished sculptor Ladislav Šaloun made the legendary chariot (triga) with the goddess Nike on the roof of the National Theatre that replaced the original one destroyed by fire. Halman also made the busts in the central hall of the National Museum. It is astonishing how elegantly and originally this 50-year-old sculptor managed to leave behind his "national artist" position to create this small, yet remarkable, artwork by the Vltava River. The bridge was finished in the spring of 1914 and, after the Sarajevo assassination in June, was named the Bridge of Archduke Franz Ferdinand. However, this name, which was politically motivated, did not take root since the crown prince was not very popular and, what's more, was associated with the outbreak of WW I. During its construction, the bridge was referred to as the New Bridge by Rudolfinum. In 1920, it was definitely renamed the Bridge of Mánes.

The fountain with dolphins by the Church of St. Nicholas at the Old Town Square was made as a virtue out of necessity. It was to stop the piling of the rubble from under-construction Pařížská Street. This inconspicuous sculpture of Rudolf Kříženecký is surrounded with a simple Cubist grille probably designed by Josef Chochol.

6 The Fountain with Dolphins by the Church of St. Nicholas

Prague 1–Old Town
Old Town Square

As the redevelopment of the Prague district of Josefov at the turn of the 19th and 20th centuries advanced, it gave rise to a Parisian-type boulevard in the northwestern part of the Old Town Square. Its original name, Mikulašská Street, was changed in 1926 to Pařížská Street. The construction of the boulevard generated tons of rubble and waste, which was piled up by the foot of the Church of St. Nicholas. To revitalize this area, it was decided to place there a Neo-Renaissance fountain, which was designed by architect Rudolf Kříženecký and built in 1906.

The sandstone, trefoil-shaped fountain was adorned in the middle with a little column holding three intertwined dolphins made by 25-year-old **Jan Štursa** (1880—1925), the founder of Czech modern sculpture. The simple Cubist grille around the fountain is a tasteful complement, although it is rather surprising for this area. It was made in 1912 and is credited to architect and builder **Josef Chochol**, one of the young architects working for the Construction Office of the Prague City Council.

Jan and Zdena Decastello's Building

Prague 1–Lessor Town
Karmelitská Street 26/268

This apartment building replaced a good-quality Baroque house that was demolished in 1904 as part of the widening of Karmelitská Street toward the Lessor Town Square due to heavy traffic. What is interesting here is that even the new commercial building right in the center of the Lessor Town was adorned with then controversial, and mostly rejected, Cubist elements. The façade of the apartment building was most likely designed by **Emil Králíček**, one of the most accomplished pioneers of the new style. The houses below Vyšehrad designed by Emil Králíček were built during the same time period and are rightfully considered the most radical examples of Cubist architecture in the world.

First, it seemed that there would be no problem to construct this building in the Lessor Town. The Construction Office approved the bold adornment — a diamond-shaped border around the windows on the third floor — but revoked the permit at the last minute in March 1913. In spite of that, the architect managed to incorporate many Cubist elements in the building.

Jan and Zdena Decastello's apartment building is standing in the row of houses that connected the two almost hermetically separated parts of the Lessor Town. The decision to demolish old houses was very painful, yet the only possible solution to replace a narrow and dark passage with a wide street. On the new building, Emil Králíček placed then controversial and now admired Cubist elements.

8 The Corner Building in the So-Called "Keys" Opening

Prague 1–Lessor Town
Karmelitská Street 30/270

Because of the plan to provide tramway transportation between the Prague suburb of Smíchov, the Lessor Town Square and the Prague district of Holešovice, it was necessary to demolish a lot of historical buildings. In spite of angry protests, the Construction Office decided to remove three houses in the southern part of the Lessor Town Square and four houses in Karmelitská

Ludvík Kysela (1883–1960)

Street creating a wedge-shaped bottleneck and forming a dark narrow pedestrian street that led to the Lessor Town Square.

The demolition was carried out in three stages during the years of 1896—1912. Four medieval houses were taken down first; two of them — one at the Lessor Town Square and one in Karmelitská Street — were called the House of the Keys, and this is why people started calling this major project the "Keys" Opening. A horse-drawn tramway started transporting people there in the first half of 1901 and a regular tramway in June of the same year. Regardless of major objections, the Renaissance Hrachov house was demolished in 1904 and the original redevelopment plans began to materialize. During the years of 1912—1913, new buildings were constructed only in some part of the opening so that entire Karmelitská Street would be of the same width.

The corner building was designed by **Ludvík Kysela** (1883—1960), one of the most prominent architects of modern Prague and to this day recognized author of elegant, technically sophisticated and clearly timeless buildings. This native from Kouřim was the younger brother of famous painter František Kysela, who made the mosaic in the rosette of the St. Vitus Cathedral at the Prague Castle and regularly collaborated

The Lessor Town demolition entered the history of Prague as the "Keys" Opening, referring to the first two Houses of the Keys that were taken down. A wide street, as a moderate version of Parisian boulevards, was to be built along the left bank of the Vltava River and to connect Smíchov with the Lessor Town Square and Holešovice by tram. This was a true catastrophe for the longtime locals.

with architects Pavel Janák and Josef Gočár. Ludvík Kysela was more interested in architecture than in painting, studied at the State Technical University in Prague under professor Josef Schulz and worked at the Construction Office in Prague. Before WW I, when the Art Nouveau style was at its peak, he discovered and was totally mesmerized by Cubist architecture and constructed the corner building of the Lessor Town Square in this architectural style. He was evidently aware of the importance of this location and also sensed the mood of the people who took a long time to get used to the open space toward Petřín Hill. In spite of that, he incorporated several Cubist details in the Late Art Nouveau decoration of the façade. The conservatives of the Society for the Protection of Old Prague became livid: *"We always insist on the postulate of artistic respect for the existing and immediate architectural surrounding and on the purity and logic of an artistic idea as well as of a system of forms."* Luckily for the admirers of Cubist architecture, Kysela's "experiment" has survived. It also shows that if it had not been for the forthcoming war, Prague could have boasted with more Cubist edifices.

9 The Czechoslovak Legions Bank (Legiobanka)

Prague 1–New Town
Na Poříčí Street 24/1046

In the fall of 1919, the commanders of the Czechoslovak Army decided to establish a financial and economic center for Czech legionaries from Russia, France and Italy where they could safely deposit their leftover salary and money from sold food rations. The bank, which was getting rich quickly, resided first in the Štefanik barracks in the Prague district of Smíchov and then moved to the hotel called U Saského dvora at the corner of Hybernská Street and Senovážná Street. In 1921, the bank called for tenders for the construction project of a new building on the land left from the demolished building that had housed probably the first Prague cabaret and brewery U Bucků. As expected, the winning design was submitted by the most accomplished architect **Josef Gočár**, who was surely very well aware of his chance to demonstrate the possibilities of the so-called national style on a monumental building in the center of Prague. Back then, many architects were literally obsessed with the search for a purely Czech version of Cubism that softened and rounded the typical Cubist sharp edges, cubes and cones in the spirit of Slavic tradition. It did not occur to them at all that they could end up in a blind alley, and actually they did not even come to an agreement regarding the standard name for this architectural style. In fact, the name has not been established to this day and all its versions — Rondo-cubism, Curve Cubism, the Legiobanka style, National Ornamentalism, Czech Art Deco or the third Cubist style — sound rather awkward. This shows that even nowadays, art historians are not sure what to do with this Czech architectural style. Josef Gočár approached the Legiobanka project in a very responsible way, thinking through every detail and symbolically combining white and brown-red marble. His vision materialized in a five-storey building with a mansard, which was strikingly bulky in spite of its rather narrow façade. He placed a huge cornice above the beautiful tripartite gate of the main entrance and used semi-columns, roundels and brown-yellow arched cornices above the windows to create the façade. His peers noticed right away that the building looked very much like a children's wooden set of blocks. The robust sculptural adornment resembling Antique triumphal arches was surprising, but evidently satisfied the taste of the stakeholder. It was made by the architect's friends and other excellent artists. Otto Gutfreund's sandstone relief showing the success and homecoming of Czech legionaries fighting for the future Czechoslovak independent state is on the ledge of the second storey. Jan Štursa's four sculptures of legionaries with the names of the battlefields on the Austrian, French and Italian fronts are atop the pillars of the main entrance.

The interior was also dominated with cylindrical, circular and semi-circular motifs. Josef Gočár admitted that the three-nave hall of the bank vestibule had been modeled after the Postal Savings Bank in Vienna from 1912, where accomplished architect Otto Wagner had beautifully combined glass and steel. The ceiling and wall paintings in the national colors were made by the architect's friend František Kysela and so was the stained glass in front of the trifoliate vault of the magnificent skylight above the bank hall. The best preserved original adornment is in the column hall of the waiting room on the first floor, in the so-called columbarium. Gočár also designed the furniture, lighting, railing ironwork, elevator grille and doorknobs. In the basement was a concert hall with an organ, which was later on converted into a theatre where the D34 Theatre of Emil František Burian performed.

This edifice is a wonderful example of Rondocubism, often also called the Legiobanka style. It became a model for several other buildings in former Czechoslovakia as well as a long-lasting target of all opponents of this "unnatural" national style who claimed that only international architecture had a future. In truth, Rondocubism as an artistic style soon outlived itself and disappeared for good after the year of 1925.

The new "national style" was characterized by a system of circular sectors and cylindrical wedges, which for instance Josef Gočár used so rigorously that his buildings resembled a children's wooden set of blocks. His Legiobanka is a remarkable edifice, which even gave this style its name, but its individual details are apparently more spectacular than the overly decorated building.

10   Teacher Houses

Prague 1–Old Town
Elišky Krásnohorské Street
10/123, 12/1021, 14/1037

Two town houses and one corner house with an L-shaped ground-plan replaced the predominantly Renaissance House of the Three Silver Stars in the redevelopment zone of the Old Town and Josefov at the end of the transformation of this area. For this construction project, the Association for the Construction of Teacher Houses in Prague hired 40-year-old foremost Czech architect **Otakar Novotný** (1880—1959), who surprisingly had resisted the avant-garde style for a long time but ended up falling for it. These houses from the years of 1919—1921 were his most important Cubist project and entered the history of architecture as the last major piece of Prague architecture from the era when Cubism was still admired and in demand. Their façade was divided with the typical Cubist elements, such as slicing planes between four-storey buildings, balconies, chess-like bays with ledges and cornices, decorations between windows, triangular attic gables and framed shop windows. Each entrance had the typical diamond-shaped vault and metal wrought grille. The hallways and staircases inside were also decorated with Cubist details and ornaments. The architect simply thought of everything, making sure that his overall vision would be fulfilled.

Prominent Czech architect Otakar Novotný (1880—1959) was one of Jan Kotěra's most talented pupils. He resisted for a long time the challenges of Cubist architecture since he principally rejected all purposeless experiments. However, despite that, he is credited with several Cubist buildings in Prague. He designed for instance the traffic control tower and the water tower at the airport in Kbely. For his contribution to architecture, he received many awards, including the French Order of the Legion of Honor.

Otakar Novotný gained his experience from the architectural elite. He worked in the studio of Josef Schulz and studied under professor Jan Kotěra, who he replaced in 1923 as an external professor of the Academy of Fine Arts. After that, he worked as a regular professor of architecture at the Academy of Arts, Architecture and Design and, before WW II, became its president. For many years, he was the chairman of the Mánes Association of Fine Artists and received many awards and decorations, including the French Order of the Legion of Honor. Before abandoning Cubism for good, he designed another Cubist residential house in Prague 7, about which we will talk later, as well as another four buildings, including the traffic control tower and the water tower at the airport in the Prague district of Kbely.

The so-called Teacher Houses in Elišky Krásnohorské Street were built during the last phase of Josefov's redevelopment. Architect Otakar Novotný, who was not one of the avant-garde enthusiasts, finally succumbed to this style since it was very much in demand at that time. Both buildings were in fact the last important project realized in the Cubist style. They were originally built in a narrow street, but did not lose any of their artistic value when the area was opened up in the 1960s due to the construction of Hotel InterContinental.

11 The Trade Union Building

Prague 1–Old Town
Na Perštýně Street 11/347

This apartment building with offices and meeting rooms was commissioned by the Czechoslovak Trade Union Association and built at the place of demolished medieval houses during the years of 1920–1922. The monumental edifice was designed by **Alois Dryák** (1872–1932), a pupil of Prof. Friedrich Ohmann who was the leading architect of Czech Art Nouveau. It is now deemed as a remarkable, and in a way admirable, attempt of the almost 50-year-old architect to materialize the ideas of the second phase of Czech Cubism. The twelve window centerlines were adorned with Cubist elements. The Cubist pillars of the main entrance, which created the pedestal for four huge stone statues representing different professions, were made by an unknown sculptor.

Alois Dryák was once a very reputable architect. Although one of his buildings, Archduke Stephan Hotel (later called Šroubek Hotel and today Europe Hotel) at Wenceslas Square is a wonderful example of Czech Art Nouveau, he became famous for his architectural concept of two of the most famous Prague monuments. He made a wooden copy of the Saint Wenceslas statue designed by Myslbek and placed it in different suggested locations to find the best one, which turned out to be Wenceslas Square. The exact location of the František Palacký statuary at František Palacký Square was the subject of long discussions as well because it was not feasible to align it with the bridge centerline as originally planned.

The Post Office and Telegraph Employees Building, better known as the Radio Palace, was designed by Alois Dryák in the fading-away national version of Cubism. The building looks somewhat timid in Vinohradská Street, the major roadway of the Prague district of Královské Vinohrady.

12 The Radio Palace

Prague 2–Vinohrady
Vinohradská Street 40/1789

The Post Office and Telegraph Employees Building, known as the Radio Palace, was built during the years of 1922—1925 as a prestigious social and cultural center.

Alois Dryák
(1872–1932)

The building was designed in the Rondocubist style, also called the national style, by **Alois Dryák**. Thanks to its timelessness and functionality and the architect's refined taste, the Radio Palace has become one of the paramount edifices of the "founding fathers." The appropriate use of construction elements, the concept and color of the façade as well as the elegantly adorned interior only prove this.

The Radio Palace in the Prague district of Vinohrady is rightfully considered the last example of the fading-away national Cubism, yet is often and incomprehensibly overshadowed by other similar buildings.

13 The Adria Palace

Prague 1–New Town
Jungmannova Street 31/36
and also Národní Street 40/36

In the 1920s, the State Regulatory Commission recommended to demolish the Thun Palace in Jungmannova Street, providing a rather curious explanation: it supposedly blocked the view of the famous Gothic Church of Our Lady of the Snow. The vacant land was bought by the Italian insurance company Riunione Adriatica di Sicurtŕ. The Prague City Council set down very strict conditions for the new construction and this is probably why the insurance company picked **Josef Zasche**, the most famous Prague architect of German origin. However, his design was not approved and therefore tenders were called in 1922. **Pavel Janák** won the tender even though his design included some of Zasche's ideas.

The building was constructed during the years of 1922–1925 in the then fashionable architectural style of national Rondocubism. The palace of a trapezoidal ground-plan had eight floors, two staircases and a paternoster. The façade was adorned with stylized floral motifs, circular and triangular cornices and discs between the windows. The upper floors — as if receding — gave an impression of huge towers with battlements, looking almost like those on Renaissance palaces in Northern Italy. Many people actually think that since the stakeholders were Italians, Pavel Janák purposely made a reference to the famous Gothic Palazzo Pubblico in Florence, one of the most beautiful palaces

---

Throughout the years, the admired as well as cursed Adria Palace at the corner of Jungmann Street and Národní Street fell into and out of oblivion. Medieval architecture experts agree that architect Pavel Janák catered to the Italian stakeholders and modeled this building after Renaissance aristocratic residences in Northern Italy, in particular the spectacular Gothic Palazzo Pubblico in Florence. Yet, the Adria Palace is still waiting for its rightful place in the history of European architecture.

in Italy. The portal from Jungmannova Street was beautified with Karel Dvořák's marble statues of the Sailor with a steamboat, symbolizing Trieste, and the Reaper with a miniature Powder Tower, symbolizing Prague. The façade of the second floor was decorated with Bohumil Kafka's sculptures representing the gods Mercury, Perun, Demeter and Parca. The terrace from Národní Street was adorned with marble statues of young girls made by Otto Gutfreund. The metal statuary Adria, also called Sailing, made by Jan Štursa was installed on the Roman cornice in the middle of the façade. It is probably the biggest galvanoplastic statue in the world, a technological one-of-a-kind piece of work.

The interior of the building was very plush — Austrian pink-brown marble paneling, shiny brass on the walls and lamps and a marble mosaic on the floor in the then usual red-blue-white combination.

Even though the Adria Palace is deemed as a pure example of national Rondocubism and its architect tried to respect the style of Prague architecture, the young promoters of Functionalism criticized it left and right. They called it a "gaudy cake" ruined by too many ingredients, and so people started looking at it as a tasteless sponge cake. Le Corbusier, a Swiss architect, town planner, painter and the founder of modern architecture, saw the almost finished Adria Palace when he was in Prague to give lectures in the Mozarteum across the street. He described the building with slight disdain as a *"massive construction in the Assyrian style."* On the other hand, it is likely that the palace inspired Rudolf Steiner in creating his theory on anthroposophical architecture since he also gave lectures in the Mozarteum at the end of the 1920s.

According to available documentation, the residential and commercial building with the famous Prague pastry shop "U Myšáka" was reconstructed based on the design of Josef Gočár. The posh atmosphere and František Myšák's noted marzipan cakes and caramel sundaes brought in many clients, including such celebrities as Ema Destinová, Růžena Nasková and Oldřich Nový; even President Tomáš Garrigue Masaryk and President Edvard Beneš enjoyed his desserts.

94

14 Myšák's House

Prague 1–New Town
Vodičkova Street 31/710

Josef Gočár, the founder of so-called National Ornamentalism, did not stick with this style for a long time. Being a very strong and talented person, he had to end up with an avant-garde style, whether Constructivism or Functionalism. For the sake of completeness, let's just add that in the 1920s, he designed several other buildings in the Legiobanka style — the Bank of Brno (Jindřišská Street 15, Prague 1) and the Anglo-Czechoslovak Bank (Hybernská Street 5, Prague 1). He also built branch offices in Hradec Králové, Pardubice and Ostrava and apartment buildings for the Anglo-Czechoslovak Bank.

The reconstruction of the commercial and residential house for renowned Prague confectioner Josef Myšák was a challenge for Josef Gočár since the building owner tried quite a few different architects during the 1920s before color blueprints of the Rondocubist façade were submitted for approval. Although the documents were signed by architect Josef Čapek, it is highly probable that Josef Gočár designed the building because the stakeholder mentions this fact in his memoirs and also because his family kept Gočár's design of the face wall for a long time. Regarding the design, the Prague City Council said the following on 6 September 1922:

> *"The façade, which was approved, shall be created in a usual fashionable way, in the most modern style (Gočár — Janák), and made of artificial stone of the gray-red color."*

The plastic face wall, which was finished within one year, was topped with round gables and divided with semi-columns. The entire façade and the door were covered with roundels, cylinders and other Rondocubist elements. This unique contribution to the world-known phenomenon — Prague Cubist architecture — was actually made in a much purer style than the famous Legiobanka.

15 The John Hus House Called Kalich

Prague 1–New Town
Jungmannova Street 9/22

Bohumír Kozák
(1885–1978)

This medieval house underwent a major Renaissance and Baroque reconstruction. The credit for its very major transformation in 1923 goes to **Bohumír Kozák** (1885—1978) who grew up in a Czech Brethren family in Čáslav. During his entire life, he followed a specific system of values, thanks to which he also obtained a lot of commissions from the Evangelic Church of the Czech Brethren. He studied at the Czech Technical University in Prague under professor Josef Schulz. His work was first influenced by Ornamental Cubism before he switched to Functionalism. He collaborated with the Society for the Protection of Old Prague, pushing forth e.g. the project of the Strahov tunnel instead of the proposed Lessor Town tunnel and managing to save the natural riverbanks of Kampa Island. His opinions and viewpoints helped to get this society out of its social isolation since it was viewed as a bunch of loud old-timers.

Authorized by the six-member synod council of the Evangelic Church of the Czech Brethren, the architect added three floors to the building, divided it with a decorative Cubist cornice and adorned the sexpartite façade with Cubist elements. Even though it is not any epoch-making edifice of artistic avant-garde, it reflects the style of that time and honest work on one of the busiest streets of Prague.

The John Hus House called Kalich in Jungmannova Street was commissioned by the Evangelic Church of the Czech Brethren. In the 1930s, the synod council asked Bohumír Kozák to reconstruct the original building and to add a courtyard wing. The architect decorated the façade with inconspicuous Cubist elements that tastefully corresponded with the statue of John Hus made by sculptor Ladislav Kofránek.

16 Cubist Stand

Prague 1–New Town
Vrchlický Park, Bolzanova Street

Designed in the Rondocubist style most likely by **Pavel Janák**, this wooden tobacco and newspaper stand was built in the 1920s. It was added to the Central List of Czech Cultural Heritage on 3 May 1958. In 1980, the stand was to be taken down but was luckily saved by enthusiasts of the Prague Center for National Heritage Preservation and

Nature Protection. A year later, it was declared cultural heritage and reconstructed to its original state.

The Cubist stand is probably one-of-a-kind in the world. Its time period and style correspond with the wooden houses designed by Josef Gočár for the airport in the Prague district of Kbely.

The wooden Cubist stand, which was most likely designed by architect Pavel Janák, has been selling newspapers and tobacco for more than a century. Many times, the stand came close to being taken down when nearby Wilson Railway Station (today's Prague Main Railway Station) was "modernized," but was always salvaged. In 1980, it was reconstructed to its original state. It is perhaps the only one of its kind in the world.

Vyšehrad

Residential Building

Prague 2–Vyšehrad
Neklanova Street 2/56

This residential building with Cubist elements was designed by Josef Chochol during the years of 1912—1913. Even though his signature is not on any of the blueprints, his authorship is more than obvious if we compare it with other similar buildings below the Vyšehrad rock. This inconspicuous three-storey building had a five-axial face wall. The architect placed two balconies above the entrance and tilted out the multi-faceted "crystalline" walling with star reliefs under the roof cornice.

The building is officially credited to well-recognized Prague builder **Antonín Belada**, who also designed e.g. the Medical Institute of Charles University in Albertov, the Faculty of Philosophy by Rudolfinum and the Letná tunnel.

This corner residential building is one of the admired Cubist buildings in the Prague district of Vyšehrad, although — unlike other buildings in its vicinity — it probably will not draw the attention of Cubist enthusiasts. It is officially the work of Prague architect Antonín Belada but its overall concept and adornment suggest that it was designed by Josef Chochol.

18 Triplex House

Prague 2–Vyšehrad
Rašín Riverfront 6/42, 8/47, 10/71

This pivotal and very expensive piece of modern Czech architecture was created during the years of 1912—1913 in a seemingly bad location, right under the Vyšehrad rock near the Vltava River. But there was a reason for it. Not even this area was spared of the fashionable redevelopment, and the groomed riverfront, just a few dozens of meters from the Vyšehrad tunnel, was literally begging for a new development. The architects, who were connected to well-informed municipal officials, realized that this location would become a residential district for the wealthy crème de la crème and this would be their great chance.

The original blueprints of the triplex house vanished forever in the 1980s, but the press and correspondence of that time prove without any doubt that they were made by **Josef Chochol**. Prague builders František Hodek, Josef and Jan Bayer and Antonín Belada as well as other stakeholders, including their lawyer and construction counsel, took a certain risk with this expressive Cubist project. Nevertheless, they gave the architect a free hand and even agreed with his idea to build a complicated, yet well-balanced, house that would resemble a Baroque palace but would not overshadow the majestic Vyšehrad fortress.

The house was designed based on the Classicist concept, which means that the middle section was one storey higher than the two symmetrical "wings" and was topped with a polygonal gable. Unfortunately, sometime later its tympanum was adorned with a tasteless relief of Lumír and Princess Libuše. One part of the first storey with the balcony atop was markedly extended over the central entrance. To make it more interesting, the architect chose slanting planes, skewed supports and plastic cones. The mansard windows were placed in a typical Cubist border. The interior was designed in a rather conventional, right-angled fashion without any somewhat impractical slanting.

For the sake of completeness, let's add that architect and pastor Jan Rosůlka and his sister and famous actress Marie Rosůlková lived in this house.

The triplex house on Rašín Riverfront below the Vyšehrad rock rightfully attracts Prague visitors and can be easily compared with the architectural monuments in the Prague center. Most guidebooks actually say that this triplex house near the Vltava River was built in the pure Cubist style. Although the original blueprints do not exist anymore, the triplex house definitely reflects Josef Chochol's architectural creativity.

19 The Family House of Bedřich Kovařovič

Prague 2–Vyšehrad
Libušina Street 3/49

The blueprint of this third important Vyšehrad building from the years of 1912—1913 is the only one signed by **Josef Chochol**. It was commissioned by Ing. Bedřich Kovařovič, a construction inspector for the Prague City Council, and built on the land left from the old Schwarzenberg brickyard demolished in 1904. The architect made use of its interesting irregular ground-plan to design the house and its adjacent garden as a dynamic unit. He "covered" the three-storey villa and its hip roof with "crystalline" shapes and made a conic border around the windows with a great view of the city.

This villa with its multi-faceted, five-axial face wall toward Libušina Street is a textbook example of radical Cubism. According to Karel Čapek, the stakeholder requested *"large and rigid"* facets. The face wall was to give passers-by the impression that it was turning after them. The beautiful back façade led to the garden with the Cubist fence forming the corner of Rašín Riverfront and Vnislavova Street. Unfortunately, it was pushed back when the riverbank road was expanded, which corrupted the original plan. The semi-circular terrace in front of the back façade was connected to the garden below through five sets of stairs, each comprising of five steps.

Kovařovič's villa is rightfully considered a masterpiece of Cubist architecture and, together with its landscaped garden, is on the National List of Cultural Heritage.

The Vyšehrad villa built for construction inspector Ing. Bedřich Kovařovič enjoys the reputation of the best Cubist building of architect Josef Chochol. His imagination, obviously influenced by Braque's and Picasso's paintings, materialized in the typical "crystalline" shapes creating a remarkable play of light and shadow, which enhanced the unique dynamics of the building. After WW II, Kovařovič's villa was insensitively reconstructed. The metal fence, constituting an integral part of the garden designed in the Cubist style, was moved back due to the expansion of the riverbank road, which compromised the entire original concept. Luckily, the whole building has been brought back to its original state.

20 The Apartment Building of František Hodek

Prague 2–Vyšehrad
Neklanova Street 30/98

A picture of this impressive, original Cubist building is perhaps in every book on the history of architecture. Even from the world point of view, it is the best of the best. František Josef Hodek, a longtime supporter of architect **Josef Chochol**, was its stakeholder and builder and the co--author of the blueprints. The architect made the first sketches in the fall of 1913 and the building was finished in April of the following year. At the last minute and with the consent of the Construction Office of the Capital City of Prague where he worked, he changed the original façade, which had been designed in the sober geometric Art Nouveau style. The sought-after 30-year-old architect was evidently trying to free himself from what he had learned at the Academy of Fine Arts in Vienna.

In comparison to other architects of that time, such as Pavel Janák, Josef Gočár and Vlastislav Hofman, Josef Chochol was definitely the most radical in his search for the "new art." His buildings were free of any ornaments. He formulated his direction in his article for the magazine Style in 1913:

> *"Ornamentalism does not befit the busy lifestyle of our times that prefer the curious and suggestive asperity and the effective simplicity of the internal concentration of matter. (…) We do not want to spoil the precious, pure and smooth effect of a modern piece of architecture, both rigid and fantastic, by unbearable stumbling over many little ornaments and details that leave us indifferent."*

Chochol's Cubist period was short-lived. There are only a few Cubist buildings designed by him; however, every one of them is an architectural masterpiece. There was a reason why he did not receive many commissions. According to art and architecture historian Prof. PhDr. Rostislav Švácha, architect Josef Chochol was talented but very restless and neurotic, and dealing with him was rather complicated. His reputation of a trouble-maker is also proven true by his switching from one art association to another and his expulsion from the Mánes Association of Fine Artists due to his "national irresponsibility." He quickly and categorically changed his opinions and stubbornly insisted on the philosophy of architecture that was not dependent on external demands. Unfortunately, due to his quickly changing views on the functionality of buildings, he lost his eminent position among his peers and became a mere "textbook" authority for the young generation. And so his major contribution to Czech architecture comes only from the period of time when he was shortly interested in Cubism.

Luckily, the building was constructed by enlightened builder František Josef Hodek. It had many particularities that immediately captured people's attention. First of all, it was built on a slope at the corner of Neklanova Street and Přemyslova Street that formed an acute angle and thus evoked a magnificent ship ashore. The sharp edges of the façade gave the building tension, which was amplified by the tall slender axial pillar penetrating the huge crown cornice that boldly leaned out toward the street. The pillar seemed to be taken straight out of a Late Gothic church and its multi-faceted edges resembled a piece of a vault. Based on the design, the top of the pillar was to be adorned with a "crystalline" vase and the chimneys were to be modeled after the legendary Cubist streetlamp by the backside of Adam's Pharmacy at Jungmann Square. The multi-faceted "crystalline" shapes between the windows turned the façade into a fascinating play of light and shadow. It is strange that Josef Chochol in theory insisted on architecture without ornaments, yet in practice contradicted himself by designing Hodek's building as one giant Cubist ornament, including the Cubist entrance door with doorknobs and the interior staircase railing.

This apartment building at the corner of Neklanova Street and Přemyslova Street was built by František Josef Hodek based on the design of Josef Chochol. It was considered the symbol of Prague Cubist architecture already before WW I. It resembled a beautiful ship ready to defy time. Surprisingly, the building has never quite been finished.

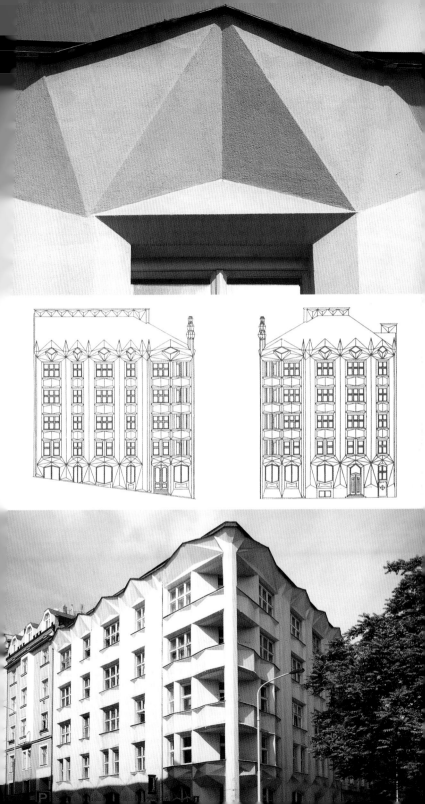

21 Mrázek's Villa "Na Libušince"

Prague 2–Vyšehrad
Rašín Riverfront 26/50

The building in the classicizing Art Nouveau style with Cubist elements was commissioned by MUDr. Vojtěch Mrázek and built during the years of 1912—1914 based on the design of architect **Emil Králíček**. This two-storey villa built on the ground-plan of an irregular triangle had a mansard roof and an adjacent ground-floor wing. The southern façade facing the crossroads of Libušina Street and the riverfront had a triangular gable with a relief of the horn of plenty and the inscription Na Libušince made by sculptor Antonín Waigant. The beautifully designed interior staircase in the Cubist style with a metal railing, original lighting and a window leading to the garden is worth noticing. Another interesting thing was a small fountain on the garden wall with a flat cover. Water poured from the spouts in the shape of a stylized human head into two spill bowls and the basin below.

This Art Nouveau building adjoins the house that Otakar Novotný built in the Kotěra modern style as well as the radical Cubist villa designed by Josef Chochol. Back then, everything was allowed and was developing, without apparently having any major impact on each other.

Mrázek's villa is a great example of the confusion of that era.

What makes Mrázek's villa "Na Libušince" so exceptional is its interior staircase with a metal railing, original lighting and a window, which is probably the only staircase in the pure Cubist style that still exists.

These three adjacent houses were designed in a very different architectural style, but give an impression of a homogenous entirety. It is a pity that they were built in an inconspicuous place between Rašín Riverfront and Libušina Street under the Vyšehrad rock.

Letná, Holešovice and Troja

22 The Bridge of Hlávka

Prague 7–Holešovice

A difficult traffic situation at the beginning of the last century forced the Prague City Council to also deal with the urgent shortage of bridges over the Vltava River. Therefore, the railway bridge below Vyšehrad was completely modernized, the wooden Libeň Bridge was built in 1902 after Libeň was annexed to Prague and the Bridge of Čech was constructed in 1908 as a result of the redevelopment of the Jewish Town. There would have been no rush to build another bridge right away, had it not been for several new circumstances. Because of floods, it became necessary to regulate the river flow, and it was also decided to build a small hydro-electric power plant on Štvanice Island. However, the main reason for building a new bridge was the strict law that came into effect at the end of the 19th century and prohibited cattle slaughtering in the city center. Therefore, a central slaughter house was set up in Holešovice and cattle were to be transported there across the new bridge.

The twelfth Prague bridge was built at the place of the strategic river crossing used by all merchants from Western Europe since the early Middle Ages. The owner of the island purposely dragged out the negotiations and made exorbitant demands, knowing well that the Prague City Council would have to yield in the end. For some unknown reasons, the construction of the bridge was split up between two architects and two contractors and carried out in two stages during the years of 1909—1912. Those who preferred traditional steel structures could not come to an agreement with those who were for modern reinforced concrete structures, and therefore they compromised. The shorter, 100-meter-long, section of the bridge from Těšnov to Štvanice Island was designed by Jiří Soukup with the architectural cooperation of Mečislav Petrů. It was made of steel parts and covered with Australian oak paving.

In charge of the longer section, which spanned partly the island and mainly the river, was 27-year-old **Pavel Janák**, a well-recognized archi-

---

The Bridge of Hlávka, which is the twelfth bridge of the Vltava River, was officially opened on 6 February 1912. It was reconstructed several times, but has never lost its obvious quality. It is not all that important whether or not it strictly corresponds with the principles of Cubist architecture.

tecture theoretician and the author of many interesting designs that, however, were never implemented. Back then, he worked as a contract architect of the Bridge Department of the Construction Office of the Capital City of Prague, was interested in weirs and had a very different idea about how the Bridge of Hlávka should look. He and Ing. František Mencl succeeded in pushing forth the reinforced concrete structure, which was considered "ugly" and therefore should be covered with stone. Pavel Janák argued that the so-far used materials and structures were nothing but a dictation absurdly determining the style and aesthetics of constructions. He expressed his opinion on this topic in his manifesto *Od moderní architektury k architektuře* [From Modern Architecture to Architecture] published in 1910.

His creative revolt was a success. The seven bridge arches, even though still largely in the Art Nouveau style, had an elegant wavelike line. The architect paid a lot of attention to the artistic decoration of the bridge and therefore asked sculptors Bohumil Kafka and Ladislav Kofránek, pupils of Josef Václav Myslbek, to make two-and-a-half-meter reliefs on the concrete walling at the top of the island pillars. The 12 medallions on both ends of each main arch represent the city councilors involved in the bridge construction and caused a lot of outrage. It did not matter that they were made by renowned sculptors Otto Gutfreund and Josef Mařatka. Journalists were screaming: *"Unbelievable things the world of culture has never heard of are happening in Prague! (…) Prague city councilors are immortalized with busts that are larger than life in size on the new Bridge of Hlávka. Down with the medallions!"*

Pavel Janák argued that the medallions were part of the artistic concept and had nothing to do with politics at all, stressing the fact that the adornment was timeless and not tendentious. Seventeen years later, he was proved right. The Prague City Council decided to replace two damaged portraits of long-forgotten officials with portraits of Josef Hlávka and Pavel Janák. They were made in 1984 by academic sculptor František Häckel, whose artistic concept was perfectly in line with that of his predecessors.

On the Bubny Riverfront at the head of the bridge on the Holešovice side were two tollbooths creating separate pedestals for Jan Štursa's sculptures called "Labor" and "Humanity." From the architectural point of view, these pedestals are exceptional also because they represented the turning point in the work of Pavel Janák, who abandoned the Viennese School style to become an enthusiastic promoter of Cubism. The Bridge of Hlávka is unique for several reasons. It was the first concrete bridge in Prague. During the years of 1958—1962, it was expanded to double-size to satisfy the planned motorway, which also makes it the widest bridge. During the expansion, the steel structure was replaced with a reinforced concrete structure. We would like to add that the bridge was named after architect, builder, politician and major benefactor Josef Hlávka (1831—1908). The fact that the name of the bridge has never changed in spite of different regimes is quite a rare thing in our country.

Sculptors Bohumil Kafka and Ladislav Kofránek carved the reliefs of human bodies right into the cement walling on the top of the island pillars. This adornment disappeared when the bridge was expanded to double-size during the years of 1958—1962. In the 1980s, faithful replicas were made and installed on the original place based on a private initiative.

In 1984, this original collection of the portraits of twelve long-forgotten Prague councilors was expanded with the bust of Pavel Janák, who designed the major part of the Bridge of Hlávka. Made by academic sculptor František Häckel, the bust perfectly corresponded with the artistic concept of his predecessors.

The medallion of Josef Hlávka is also a new decoration on the bridge. Named after this prominent Czech architect and benefactor, the bridge has never changed its name, which is a great rarity among Prague bridges.

The huge sculptures called "Labor" and "Humanity" made by Jan Štursa were kept in the municipal depository for many decades. They returned to the head of the Bridge of Hlávka on the Holešovice side thanks to the efforts of the cultural community.

23 Apartment Buildings

Prague 7– Letná
Kostelní Street 16/1104
Františka Křížka Street 6/1132, 8/1133, 10/1173

Before WW I, this Letná location was one big construction site where a new posh quarter was being created in Kostelní Street, Heřmanova Street and Františka Křížka Street, referred to as backbone streets considering their importance. This area gave us several buildings in the style verging on Art Nouveau and Cubism. Even though they are not as splendid as for instance those at Vyšehrad, they still deserve our attention and admiration. Art and architecture historian Prof. PhDr. Rostislav Švácha pointedly said:

"Cubist architecture was formed at two qualitative levels. The first one includes the designs and buildings of creative architects, such as Josef Gočár, Josef Chochol, Pavel Janák and Vlastislav Hofman, which were based on a very sophisticated artistic concept and thus were more or less of the same quality. The other level represents the work of building contractors who only superficially understood the principles of Cubist architecture, which necessarily resulted in a major difference in quality."

This was a problem of many buildings not only in the Prague district of Letná but also in Holešovice and Bubeneč, which we will talk about later, as well as of some buildings in the Prague districts of Vinohrady and Žižkov. The majority of the residential buildings in Letná were commissioned to builder and occasional designer Václav Zákostelna, but mostly to architect **Bohuslav Homoláč** (1883—1962). The latter graduated from a technical high school and focused mainly on face walls, giving them the same features: vertically structured bays, horizontally continuous balconies, geometric ornaments and Cubist cornices, stars and window and door borders. He obviously did not search for anything new and during his Cubist period of 1912—1914 successfully managed to get by just with these elements. In any case, he disgraced neither Prague nor himself.

The buildings in Letná constructed in the first decades of the last century were often decorated with Cubist elements for no reason other than to show their designers' efforts to "be in."

24 The House of the Three Atlantes

Prague 7–Letná
Šmeralova Street 15/390

This building with an exceptional façade was designed by **Bohuslav Homoláč** during the years of 1913–1914. The face wall bears all the typical signs of his work, even though the large quantity of details shows that he had already abandoned the style of geometric Art Nouveau. He decorated the building with many Cubist elements, probably at the request of the builder. Between the windows of the first storey, he placed three Atlantes supporting the continuous balcony with a metal railing.

We do not know for sure who made the muscular male statues, but their artistic interpretation suggests that they came from the studio of prominent Czech-German sculptor **Franz Metzner** (1870–1919). This native from Všeruby by Pilsen became internationally famous thanks to his adornment inside the memorial, The Battle of the Nations, in Leipzig. Except for a large number of cast sculptures in the collections of the North Bohemian Museum in Liberec, his work is practically unknown or has been destroyed, such as the fountain in Liberec or the statue of Emperor Joseph II in Teplice. In Prague, he created for instance the reliefs on the edifice of the Insurance Association for the Sugar Industry in Jindřišská Street or the façade of the Vienna Banking Union in Na Příkopě Street. According to archival documents, he made sculptures for residential buildings in many different towns of the Austro-Hungarian Empire. But due to unfortunate circumstances, we do not know which ones and for whom. And so the statues on the building in Šmeralova Street in Letná will probably also remain a mystery.

A gem in the dirt, a pearl in the sea, this is how the House of the Three Atlantes in Letná was dubbed. This house with an unusual façade made by Bohuslav Homoláč is unfortunately somewhat hidden among the surrounding inconspicuous buildings. We can only guess that the three statues supporting the balcony with a metal railing were made by sculptor Franz Metzner.

The pavilion of the School of Architecture looks rather homely next to the ostentatious main building of the Academy of Fine Arts in Letná. Yet, it was built by the most prominent figures of the history of modern Czech architecture. For many years, the typical Cubist portal was credited to Josef Gočár, but it was discovered that it was a part of Jan Kotěra's original blueprints.

The School of Architecture

Prague 7–Letná
U Akademie Street 2

In 1910, **Jan Kotěra**, the founder of modern Czech architecture, was appointed a professor of the new School of Architecture at the Academy of Fine Arts in Prague, which was an excellent idea considering that he raised an entire generation of prominent Czech architects. In the early 1920s, he was given the opportunity to design a pavilion for this school. The building in the so-called rational modern style was finished by Josef Gočár in 1924 after Jan Kotěra suddenly passed away. He had to modify the project and to add another storey and large studio windows since it had become obvious that there would not be enough space. For a long time, it was believed that the typical Cubist portal was Josef Gočár's modification because Jan Kotěra was not really into the avant-garde style. Many years later, it was discovered to everybody's surprise that the main entrance had been built based on the original blueprints. It seems that at the end of his life, Jan Kotěra embraced Cubism after all.

The Residential Building for Bank Employees

Prague 7–Holešovice
Heřmanova Street 9/1119

The residential building for the employees of the Anglo-Czechoslovak Bank was designed by **Josef Gočár** in 1922 and received its final building approval just a year later. Gočár's façade stood out among the surrounding and well-constructed buildings where mostly German bank employees lived. Its bays, huge dominant cornice and unusual blue-black color made it much more interesting.

This was probably the very first time the architect steered away from the Legiobanka style that he had created and enthusiastically promoted. The building in Heřmanova Street showed his artistic courage to admit that the obstinate search for the national version of Cubism was leading nowhere and that architecture by nature is an international artistic discipline, on which one cannot force ornaments or purposeless decorations, no matter how great they look on blueprints.

The residential building for the employees of the Anglo-Czechoslovak Bank in Heřmanova Street was unlike the other buildings. In this case, architect Josef Gočár probably for the first time gave up his vision that only the national style was the right version of Cubism, which he had promoted when building his Legiobanka.

27

The Building of the Teacher Association

Prague 7–Letná
Kamenická Street 35/811

Otakar Novotný
(1880–1959)

This prestigious landmark of Prague Cubist architecture is hidden among older buildings. It was designed in the Late Rondocubist style by architect **Otakar Novotný** (1880—1959) and built in the years of 1923—1924. During his last year at the State Technical College in Prague, this native from Benešov worked in the studio of Josef Schulz and took part in the construction project of the Museum of Decorative Arts. He also studied under Jan Kotěra, who he later on replaced as a professor of the Academy of Fine Arts. He also taught at the Academy of Arts, Architecture and Design and even became its president. While retired, he gave lectures and led seminars on architectural styles and morphology. He was very actively involved in the activity of the Mánes Association of Fine Artists and became its longtime chairman.

His first buildings in the Art Nouveau style were clearly influenced by Jan Kotěra and his admiration for then popular folk architecture. During his stay in the Netherlands, he was inspired by fair-faced brickwork that he later on used on many of his modernistic buildings. In about 1912, he became interested in Cubism and designed mainly interiors in this style. It is true though that he was not part of the mainstream Czech Cubist architects. Nevertheless, during the years of 1919—1921, he tried this avant-garde style on the block of residential buildings for Prague teachers constructed on an available piece of land left from the redevelopment of the Prague district of Josefov, in today's Elišky Krásnohorské Street.

It seems that he and the stakeholder got along really well, which led to another joint project, this time in Kamenická Street. The building of the Teacher Association was a rather bold experiment where the architect forwent the Kotěra tradition and wonderfully tackled the popular "National Ornamentalism." The face wall was adorned with rounded semi-columns all the way to the third storey, which gave the entire building the feel of roundness and dynamic undulation.

We must say that in this case, the otherwise misleading term "Rondocubism" is more than appropriate. To amplify the rhythmical effect, the architect added semi-circular cornices above and under the windows. He decided against the then fashionable color distinction of individual elements and the chess-like design of the façade and instead covered the face wall with artificial stone in the national colors, which unfortunately faded with time into plain gray. This, however, does not change the fact that this building made its mark in the history of architecture as one of the purest examples of the Czech version of Late Cubism. Later on, Otakar Novotný switched to Functionalism, which we can see for instance on the building that he designed for the Mánes Association of Fine Artists on Slovanský Island by the Masaryk Riverfront in 1927—1930.

Exceptional projects required bold builders and huge investments. Therefore, it is quite surprising that the rather poor Teacher Association decided for such a project in Kamenická Street in Letná. The association probably liked the high-quality buildings of their colleagues constructed after the redevelopment of Josefov and found architect Otakar Novotný, who was able to accommodate them. He even gave the building Rondocubist features and covered the façade with artificial stone in the national colors.

The Administration Building of the Materna Factory

Prague 7–Holešovice
Dělnická Street 20/313

František Josef Materna founded the first Czech company selling lacquer and later expanded it with the production of varnish and paint. For this reason, he bought and remodeled a factory in Holešovice. When the original office and residential building became too small, he asked for help from his friend — architect, town planner and furniture designer **Rudolf Stockar** (1886–1957). Based on this architect's design, the building was expanded in the Late Cubist style during the years of 1919–1921. He made the interior and furnishings in the same style and later on furnished Materna's own villa in Střešovice with Cubist furniture as well.

Rudolf Stockar designed several buildings, especially schools in Bohemia and hospitals in Slovakia, but became internationally famous as an interior designer. He was one of the leading figures and a director of

15 years of Artěl, an association of applied arts and design workshops, which produced Cubist home accessories, vases, bowls, tea sets, ceramics, lamps, jewelry as well as furniture, fabrics and cigarette holders on a small scale. Stockar's products were always highly aesthetic, although they reflected his complicated journey from Art Nouveau to Cubism all the way to Art Deco.

He designed the one-storey administration building in Dělnická Street in a very simple way but gave it a distinct Cubist face wall, which was something very unusual in this part of Prague. In 1932, the paint production was moved to a new plant in Hostivař and is there to this day. It is too bad that banal eye-catchers are now competing with the remarkable façade made by Rudolf Stockar.

29 The Wooden Houses of Josef Gočár

Prague 7–Troja
U Trojského zámku Street 3/120

Besides the magnificent banks, such as Legiobanka, the Bank of Brno and the Anglo-Czechoslovak Bank, **Josef Gočár** also designed several provisional wooden buildings, such as the Czechoslovak stand for the international trade fair in Lyon, France, and the exhibition pavilion of the Mánes Association of Fine Artists in the courtyard of one of the buildings in Vodičkova Street. However, the wooden houses for the administration of the new Prague airport in Kbely, where the first airplanes took off in December 1918, deserve special attention. To some extent, their design mirrored the era right after the foundation of independent Czechoslovakia when a group of leading Czech architects searched for a style that would correspond with the enthusiasm about the end of WW I, the fall of the Austro-Hungarian Empire and especially the newfound freedom. The society's mood manifested itself in the so-called National Ornamentalism characterized by simple ornaments in the national colors.

The Gočár wooden houses with a double-pitched roof and very colorful discs, semi-circles and parallelograms resembled gingerbread houses. They perfectly befitted the airport, considering the very primitive airplanes of that time. One of the houses served as an inn as well as a departure and arrival hall that could seat several dozens of people. Another one was used by the foreman and the third one served as a storage room for different things, fuel included. In the same style, he designed the administration building with a branch of the Czechoslovak Customs Office for the French-Romanian Company for Air Transport that obtained the first license for long-distance flights in former Czechoslovakia. After the airport in Ruzyně was opened in April 1937, the entire civil air transport was moved there, and the airport in Kbely served the army. In the 1970s, it was decided to demolish the rather

Josef Gočár designed the wooden, distinctly decorated Cubist houses as provisional buildings for the airport in Kbely. Two of them underwent a major reconstruction and have been a useful embellishment of the ZOO in Troja since 2011.

STÁTNÍ CIV. LETIŠTĚ PRAHA.

devastated houses. Prof. Zdeněk Veselovský, an enlightened director of the Prague ZOO, was able to save the two best preserved houses. They were disassembled and put back together in the lower part of the ZOO near the Vltava River. Unfortunately, their furnishings were ruined and so were their different colors painted with dark luxol stain. These unique wooden houses were heavily damaged by the flood in 2002 and had to be moved again, this time to the northern, elevated part of the ZOO with a great view of the city skyline. They underwent a comprehensive and very expensive reconstruction, during which their missing parts were replaced and their original colors restored. In March 2011, the Gočár wooden houses were officially opened to the public as a restaurant and gallery and became one of the admired landmarks of the ZOO.

Hradčany, Dejvice and Bubeneč

30 Villas

Prague 6–Hradčany
Tychonova Street 4/269, 6/268

The biggest urban development in the vicinity of the Prague Castle in the years of 1910 — 1914 took place at the site of the bastions of St. George, St. Ludmila and St. Thomas that used to be a part of the removed Baroque fortification. Historical monument conservationists managed to save only the Písek Gate. The garden-city project was based on the romantic model promoted mainly in England and Germany. The Regulatory Department of the Construction Office of the Prague City Council oversaw that everyone followed the concept prepared by a group of young talented architects, such as **Vlastislav Hofman** and **Vladimír Zákrejs**. Nobody was sure at first whether people would be interested in such expensive land parcels, but actually, they were selling like hot cakes among notables — physicians, architects, bank and insurance company officials, builders, artists and politicians. Two of the owners were for instance President Tomáš Garrigue Masaryk and sculptor František Bílek. The homes were designed by foremost architects.

No other location has ever seen such great architects working next to each other.

In October 1911, **Josef Gočár** prepared the blueprints of the Art Nouveau duplexes for Karel Hoffmann and Jan Stach, officials of the Prague Municipal Insurance Company. His project in Tychonova Street in Hradčany was most likely approved, but the following year the architect submitted a new version with many distinct Cubist details. To this country-style villa with a mansard roof, he added Cubist supports and bay cornices on the northern and southern façades. The modern style is much more apparent on the entrances protruding from two rounded staircase areas. The high cylindrical columns on each side remotely resembled the Bohdanec water tower that he designed in 1910. The octagonal wooden gazebo with a conic roof and a dome topped with a vase was a wonderful reminder of his radical Cubist era. It is probably one-of-a-kind in the world.

Josef Gočár built the duplex in Hradčany across from the Summer House of Queen Anne in the Classical Art Nouveau style. However, as he said later on, he decorated it with so many Cubist elements that he had nothing against it being classified as Cubist architecture.

31 The Buildings of Jaroslav Vondrák

Prague 6
Čs. Armády Street 4/346 a 6/345
Dejvická Street 36/555
Bubenečská Street 51/495
Českomalínská Street 9/496, 11/527, 13/528
Západní Street 21/488 (the villa of architect Jaroslav Vondrák)
the corner of Verdunská Street and Charles de Gaulle Street
the corner of Terronská Street and Rooseveltova Street

In the late 1910s, tenders were called for the construction of villas with several two-bedroom and three-bedroom apartments for the building association of state and public employees in the Prague districts of Střešovice and Ořechovka. To avoid uniformity, it was decided to alternate town houses with single houses, based on the example of English garden-cities. Jan Šenkýř and **Jaroslav Vondrák** (1881–1937) won the tender and built this first large post-war colony of family houses. Jaroslav Vondrák, a pupil of Jan Kotěra at the

Jaroslav Vondrák
(1881–1937)

Academy of Arts, Architecture and Design, designed a market-hall, restaurant and cinema with the typical Cubist pyramid-shaped and round elements in the middle of this residential area.

Jaroslav Vondrák also built his own villa in the expressive modern style in Západní Street in Střešovice during the years of 1923–1924. Its distinct feature was the asymmetrical composition full of dynamics consisting of three parallel concepts. These forms blending together resembled beautiful ships wedged into each other, while the chimney on the very top evoked a rudder.

He designed the fair-faced apartment buildings in Bubeneč, in today's Československé armády Street, in the modern style and with Cubist elements. This is also how he beautified two corners. On the

The luxurious apartment buildings in the Prague districts of Dejvice, Bubeneč, Střešovice and Ořechovka were designed only by the most sought-after architects commissioned by very demanding stakeholders. Even though they were not the "founding fathers" of Prague Cubist architecture, they all tried to adapt to the clientele enchanted by avant-garde. Let's remember that these were not true Cubist buildings, but buildings with Cubist adornment "catering to the taste of that era."

corner where Terronská Street meets Rooseveltova Street, he built a three-storey apartment building with a façade made mostly of faced bricks arranged into different decorative Rondocubist elements. He made a fishbone strip above the windows next to the red entrance door and an open trifoliate fan above the windows of the second floor.

The other building was on the corner of Verdunská Street and Charles de Gaulle Street. While the façade of the previous building consisted of continuous brick areas, this building had only brick decorations on the otherwise smooth light parget. Above the semi-circular balconies was, of course, his favorite element — a brick triangle — as an expression of his motto: *"A brick decoration, no abomination."*

32

Apartment Building

Prague 6– Bubeneč
Národní obrany Street 4/457

This apartment building in the Late Art Nouveau style was made in 1914 based on the design of architect and builder **Jan Petrák**. The architect adorned the mansard roof, central angular section protruding to the street and triangular gable above the entrance "guarded" by two owls on each side with many Cubist elements in a very helter-skelter way. He definitely was not the only one to do so. There were many other Prague builders who similarly adapted to the fad and were rightly criticized for it by the "founding fathers," who had a difficult time searching for the new style. Back then, Josef Chochol wrote:

"The naïve copying of Cubist architecture by simple slanting, sloping, turning, skewing or any other distorting does not transform old architecture into new architecture."

Back then, many buildings were certainly built in a similar way and were later on modernized, but the apartment building in Bubeneč was left as one of the last reminders of "faux Cubist architecture."

The building in the Late Art Nouveau style in Národní obrany Street in the Prague district of Dejvice became a major target of criticism of both Cubist architecture promoters and art historians. They reproached Jan Petrák for his purposeless use of symbols, such as rectangles, squares, triangles and rosaces, to fill a free space without any deeper meaning. On the other hand, even such buildings make Prague the City of Cubism.

Other Places in Prague

33

The Big Ďáblice Cemetery

Prague 8–Ďáblice
Ďáblická Street 20/555

Prague was faced with a difficult situation at the beginning of the last century. The problem was that all cemeteries were full. There were several options as to where to build a new cemetery, and the choice fell on a vacant area in North Prague — at the borderline of Ďáblice and Střížkov. Tenders were called in 1912, and the design of **Vlastislav Hofman**, an employee of the Regulatory Department of the Construction Office of the Prague City Council, won. No wonder the complete documentation was approved within a very short period of time, the construction got immediately under way and the basic concept of the cemetery was finished before WW I broke out in 1914.

Vlastimil Hofman designed the road to the deceased as a huge doorway to the world of ashes. Two Cubist kiosks with octagonal windows and a stepped roof symbolized ash motes that the architect separated with a tripartite metal gate representing a molecular grille. All this was designed in the pure, very powerful radical Cubist style, which was generally referred to as "intently dismal." All elements seem to crystallize. This definitely was no traditional reverent place with a little church and angels. Unfortunately, after the war the municipal stakeholder abandoned Vlastimil Hofman's concept of the Ďáblice cemetery, and thus nowadays there is just a fragment of the architect's plan. Moreover, the then main gate is now a side gate and the kiosks are standing there all alone.

A remainder of a Cubist masterpiece can be found in the outskirts of Prague. This nowadays forgotten, but once main, entrance to the cemetery in Ďáblice with two kiosks on each side was one of the few architectural works of excellent stage designer Vlastislav Hofman. His grandiose project of a non-traditional mourning place definitely was put to an end by WW I.

This four-storey building with a raised ground floor and commercial premises in Husitská Street proves that Cubist architecture penetrated the blue-collar Prague district of Žižkov as well. The decorative cornices supporting the corner bay turned this otherwise ordinary building of Bohuslav Homoláč into a little gem.

34 The Čvančara Apartment Building

Prague 3–Žižkov
Husitská Street 32/753

Architect and builder **Bohuslav Homoláč**, who has already been mentioned in this book, constructed several Late Art Nouveau buildings
with Cubist elements in different Prague districts, for instance in Letná
and Vinohrady, during the years of 1912—1919. In 1913, he was faced
with a real challenge — to design a building on a trapezoidal land
parcel in Husitská Street near the Žižkov railway viaduct. In the new
version of his design, he added distinct Cubist motifs to his four-storey
building, which was initially in the Art Nouveau style and seemed to be
"mounted" over the commercial premises and raised ground floor. Very
original are especially the wedge-shaped cornices below the corner bay.
Later on, he repeated this idea on other buildings as well.

CZECH CUBISM
IN THE EUROPEAN CONTEXT

One of the reasons why tourists admire Prague so much is because they do not quite understand its esotericism. People are by and large lured and magnetized by mystery, which is also true about architecture. Cubism literally broke through the exciting compilation of architectural styles in the first decade of the last century with such speed, maturity and fierceness that it was impossible to find any followers or successors anywhere in the world. It was perhaps a combination of many circumstances, but it was definitely a historical chance to achieve something unprecedented.

A group of extraordinarily talented people born mostly around the year of 1890 and promoting the new architectural style emerged in Prague within a very short period of time. The revolutionary concept was born in a difficult and complicated way, first as a theory that later materialized in the streets and squares of the city. It was somewhat easier for painters. Emil Filla, Bohumil Kubišta, Josef Čapek, Otto Gutfreund and many others built on the ideas of the French "founding fathers" — Pablo Picasso and Georges Braque. On the other hand, Prague architects had to start from scratch. This is why especially architecture magazines published many articles where architects formalized step by step their ideas, opinions and thoughts. They all had everything that it takes to succeed: they were young (often not even 30 years old), talented, assertive and unburdened by conventions. Thanks to their very good education at the Academy of Fine Arts in Prague and in Vienna or at other universities, they had a great career ahead of them and mostly wished to establish themselves. Their names have been mentioned in this book and so let's just recall some of them: Josef Gočár, Pavel Janák, Vlastislav Hofman and Josef Chochol. Dozens to hundreds of drawings, sketches and designs demonstrate their distressful search for self-realization where they tried to incorporate the revolutionary axioms of painting into architecture, even if it was a very precarious direction.

After our virtual visitation of the Prague Cubist buildings in this book, it would be certainly good to recollect the principles of Cubism. It may seem like detective work with many possible points of departure where everybody is entitled to his own opinion. Is it true then that

Georges Braque (1882—1963) and Pablo Picasso (1881—1973)

Cubism is an independent, in some ways blind, alley of Expressionism? The fundamental principle lies in the attempt to look at an object from different angles and perspectives all at once. A viewer should have an impression of walking around an object while his eyes move all over the canvas and see specific details in unusual relationships. Colors do not mirror reality either. Paintings go beneath the surface of things to reveal the essence of the message, and this is also why they are dynamic and provide an unusual experience that is not always very easy to understand. In Cubism, the content/form correlation is rather problematic since the true message is obscured in numbers or even letters, and the story is usually depicted at several time levels.

Those who are not experts should not feel bad since even art historians have a hard time explaining this so-far last major art movement in our history. They wrote a great number of pages to finally agree in principle on several evincible phases of the Cubist development. The first phase, called **Pre-Cubism** (1906—1909), is connected with Pablo Picasso and Georges Braque. Their artwork was influenced by previous art movements and they probably discovered the innovative perspective independently from each other. They used only basic geometric forms and shades of gray and brown. The second phase — **Analytic (also Hermetic) Cubism** (1909—1912) — focused on a new perspective, a view from different angles and the dynamics of objects. The

Ossip Zadkine (1890—1967): The Destroyed City, 1953; Rotterdam

painters broke down a depicted model into individual geometric shapes to place them on the canvas next to each other in a "non-perspective way." So, it was not yet true abstract art. They did not use any bright colors, and if they did, then only with certain exaggeration. The paintings from this phase of Cubism are very expressive. The last phase, called **Synthetic (also High) Cubism** (1912—1914), approached abstract art the most, but a depicted object was still important for the painters even if they broke it down into different lines and planes and then put them back together to create a new image. They started using collage and employed bright colors. Quite logically, Cubism was not embraced just by painters but gradually also by sculptors. This is how it was in entire Europe and former Czechoslovakia as well. Probably the most spectacular Cubist sculpture, The Destroyed City, stands on a square in Rotterdam, the second largest Dutch city. It was made by famous French sculptor of Russian origin Ossip Zadkine (1890—1967) as a stylized human figure without a heart to symbolize the destruction of the Rotterdam center after several carpet bombings during WW II. In Bohemia, it was Otto Gutfreund who pioneered avant-garde sculpture of world importance. His statue "Anxiety" from 1911—1912 is considered the first genuine Cubist sculpture in the world. This naturally brings us to architecture. No matter how hard we search, Czech Cubist architects are a rarity in the world, except perhaps for French sculptor **Raymond Duchamp-Villon** (1876—

R. Duchamp-Villon and his brother Marcel Duchamp

1918), an enthusiastic organizer of regular meetings with other prominent artists and critics where they talked about interesting topics, including the new Cubist style that he liked and fiercely defended. His soul mates in this exquisite company were for instance his brothers Jacques and Marcel Duchamp, Pablo Picasso, Georges Braque, Guillaume Apollinaire, Fernand Léger and František Kupka.

Raymond Duchamp-Villon had a great vision: he wanted to build a "Cubist House" in the little village of Puteaux in the outskirts of Paris where he and his brothers worked. A model of this house, the only genuine Cubist edifice outside Bohemia, appeared in the catalog of the prestigious art exhibition in Paris — Salon des Indépendants — in 1912. When exhibiting his artwork in the Mánes Exhibition Hall in Prague a year later, he was in awe of Czech Cubist architecture, which only reassured him that he was heading in the right direction. Unfortunately, his project did not materialize. WW I broke out and he had to enlist in a mobile army hospital since he had originally studied medicine. He became infected with the typhus bacteria and died in October 1918.

The "Cubist House" in the little village of Puteaux, which is now a part of Paris's outskirts, was to be the only truly Cubist building outside our country and Prague in particular. Unfortunately, WW I put an end to sculptor Raymond Duchamp-Villon's dream. The picture of the model in the catalog of the art exhibition Salon des Indépendants from 1912 is the sole reminder of willingness to experiment. It became famous a year later when Guillaume Apollinaire mentioned it in his book *Les Peintres cubists*.

Rudolf Steiner (1861—1925), an Austrian philosopher, literary critic, artist and mostly esotericist, was another prominent person who came to understand and respect Czech Cubist architecture in the first quarter of the last century. When visiting Prague, he admired its Cubist edifices, such as the Mozarteum, the Adria Palace and the Diamond House, just as much as its Gothic and Baroque architecture.

RUDOLF STEINER AND PRAGUE CUBISM

(WRITTEN BY TOMÁŠ BONĚK)

Rudolf Steiner came to Prague twelve times during the years of 1909—1924. He gave lectures in downtown Prague — in the hall of the Merkur Trading Association in today's Pařížská Street, the Mozarteum, the Municipal House, etc. and regularly visited the salon of Berta Fantová in the House of the Unicorn at the Old Town Square. He also liked to search local second-hand book shops. It is more than likely that while taking a stroll around Prague, he examined the Cubist buildings and realized the importance of this radical new idea that he later incorporated in his own work. However, his buildings are not just some kind of imitation. While Prague Cubists deemed the sharp edge as an important architectural element, Rudolf Steiner used a curved plane as the basic form. Moreover, contrary to Czech architects, he focused first on interiors before switching to exteriors.

To get a better idea, it is necessary to realize that the turn of the 19th and 20th centuries was marked with rapid and major changes in all aspects of life. It was the time of intensive searching and experimenting. Often very antagonistic movements and points of departure clashed and influenced each other. In a way, the social, economic and artistic tornado culminated in the horrors of WW I. After the war, the world changed for good. During this dramatic period of time, many were looking for a new spiritual orientation and, in the last third of the 19th century, many artists and intellectuals surprisingly found it in the theosophy of Helena Petrovna Blavatsky (1831—1891). To this day,

---

The Goetheanum, a Swiss national monument and the seat of the Anthroposophical Society as well as of the Free University of Spiritual Science, was built based on Rudolf Steiner's design during the years of 1924—1928. His authentic artistic style is noted especially for being free of traditional architectural constraints. For awestruck Le Corbusier, it was functionalist architecture. Today, historians tend to deem it as a supreme example of Expressionism. It is strange that both Rudolf Steiner and Le Corbusier knew Prague Cubism, yet never mentioned this inspiration in any context.

The Goetheanum on the hill above Dornach, south of Basel, is surrounded with many other buildings built in the anthroposophical architectural style. This picture shows the Vreede House, the work of Rudolf Steiner and sculptor Edith Maryon.

her undeniable influence has often been trivialized. Yet, it has been proven that for instance writer Julius Zeyer and sculptor František Bílek used her ideas in their work. Helena Petrovna Blavatsky's theosophic movement was followed up on by Rudolf Steiner, whose importance for many fields of creativity has now been finally appreciated by both esotericists and exotericists. Only a few of Rudolf Steiner's contemporaries recognized the exceptional spiritual wealth of his work. Among them were for instance Albert Schweitzer, a German physician, missionary, philosopher and recipient of the Nobel Peace Prize, and then especially artists, such as Russian painter and modern abstract art theoretician Wassily Kandinsky, Dutch abstract painter Piet Mondrian, German painter of Russian origin Alexei von Jawlensky, Swedish pioneer of pure abstract art Hilma af Klint, German painter Otto Fröhlich, Cubist painter and symbolist Franz Marc, who established his own color rules, Swiss modern painter Paul Klee, Russian symbolistic writer Andrei Bely, German poet, journalist and translator Christian Morgenstern and Franz Kafka, one of the most influential writers of the last century. Of course, not all of them were Steiner's pupils, but the confrontation with his ideas was very important and fruitful for them. We must also point out that Rudolf Steiner was a very good observer of current trends and art movements and embraced, developed and perfected many of them. Time has proven that he understood the pulsation of his era. His influence probably was and still is much greater than one would imagine. In this book, we are of course mostly interested in his contribution to architecture. Architects were in fact the first to notice Rudolf Steiner's work, albeit with some delay because his major essays were not published until the 1960s. In 1920, Le Corbusier, a French painter and town planner of Swiss origin, supposedly stood awestruck in front of the in-progress Second Goetheanum, the seat of the Anthroposophical Society.

Kenji Imai, a 31-year-old Japanese professor of architecture at Waseda University in Tokyo, visited the unfinished monumental building the same year. However, he did not fully appreciate it until almost 40 years later since he was disappointed in many respects by his second trip to Europe. The only thing that impassioned him was Rudolf Steiner's building in Dornach south of Basel. After his return home, he decided to introduce Rudolf Steiner and his work in Japan and wrote:

> "I must mention here the noble ideas that Rudolf Steiner, an unknown architect and a former philosopher, psychologist and educator, will bring to our modern and future world of architecture. The building of the Free University of Spiritual Science, his principal piece of architecture, lies deep in the past. Moreover, it was overshadowed by the Bauhaus movement in Dessau that emerged before us at the end of 1926 as a leader of modern architecture. And yet, I am convinced that Rudolf Steiner's idea, which did not conform to functionalist architecture and therefore was disdainfully condemned, buried and forgotten, stands today before us strong, still, viable and forever present. I think that we should look once again at Rudolf Steiner's solemn spirit that lives in the Goetheanum. I cannot but notice his heartfelt wish to bring mankind love and harmony. (…) I must point out something curious: tradition, which plays such an important role among today's architects, means nothing in view of his work.
> I implore all architects of the world to make the Goetheanum — created by Rudolf Steiner, a great philosopher of spiritual science, mystic artist and architect — their current and modern friend and to visit this building even if only once. I wish them the chance to con-

template the value and essence of this building and to recognize what a true and dynamic building is."

It is not easy to fit Rudolf Steiner's specific piece of architecture into the movements of the last century. Expressionism was obviously the closest to his heart, but he transformed it with many other influences. The Goetheanum style is sometimes considered an "aesthetic anti-Bauhaus." Swiss architect Hannes Meyer (1889—1954) — the second director of Bauhaus, one of the most prominent avant-garde schools of art, design and architecture — was needlessly embittered, perhaps out of conceit. After all, it has been sufficiently documented that some Bauhaus artists were very much interested in theosophical-anthroposophical ideas to the great displeasure of Bauhaus leaders. In relation to this, it is often said that anthroposophy and Prague Cubism resemble each other. It is even truer about the so-called anthropologic design than architecture. Some furniture, painting frames and utility items are hard to classify without knowing the context and time of their creation but, contrary to Cubist architecture, this design style keeps developing.

The opinion of Hannes Meyer, the protagonist of the functionalist section, was unjust. He probably had no idea how deeply and thoroughly his "adversary" was interested in the issues that bothered him as well. For Rudolf Steiner, art was a social, therapeutic and educa-

These buildings have been called eurythmic ever since their construction in 1920. They housed the Goetheanum's collaborators.

This house called Duldeck was designed by Rudolf Steiner. It was origi-nally built for the family of dentist Emil Grosheintz, who donated the land on which the Goetheanum was built. The villa is considered one of the boldest buildings made of reinforced cement at the beginning of the 20th century. Nowadays, it houses the archives of Rudolf Steiner.

tional matter. He strived for a society that would create a new organic artistic style based on a new spiritual experience. He elaborated on his ideas about art and architecture in dozens of his lectures, essays and works. During the years of 1913–1925, he made over 20 buildings in Dornach that he designed either by himself or in collaboration with his close friend, English sculptor Edith Maryon (1872–1924) and then developed with other architects.

Many people have already noticed that Rudolf Steiner's thoughts about art and architecture go much farther and deeper than his com-pleted buildings created in the historical context of the first quarter of the last century. Many architects followed up on his ideas. As a result, there are thousands of school buildings, clinics, therapeutic-educa-tional facilities, churches and residential buildings constructed in the style of organic architecture inspired by Rudolf Steiner in more than 40 countries around the world. We can also see the resemblance with the Prague Cubist school when we consider that both architectural movements were forgotten for many years. The world in the 1930s simply and definitely set off in a different direction.

BIBLIOGRAPHY

- *Bilder einer Metropole, Die Impressionisten in Paris*, Museum Folkwang, Essen, 2010
- Boněk Jan: *Židovská Praha* [Jewish Prague], Eminent, Prague, 2009
- Diviš Vladimír: *Apollinaire a Čechy* [Apollinaire and Bohemia], Český fond výtvarných umělců, Prague, 1961
- Dudáček Lubomír: *Dopravní letiště Prahy* [Prague Airports], MBI, Prague, 1998
- Fäth Reinhold J.: *Dornach Design*, Futurum Verlag, Dornach, 2011
- Ganteführer-Trier Anne: *Cubism*, Taschen, 2004
- *Jubilejní výstava v Praze* [The Jubilee Exhibition in Prague], exhibition committee, Prague, 1891
- Kiesling Norbert: *Pavel Janák*, Arbor vitae, Řevnice, 2011
- *Kubistická Praha* [Cubist Prague], Středočeská galerie a nakladatelství, Prague, 2004
- Lahoda Vojtěch: *Český kubismus* [Czech Cubism], Brána, Prague, 1996
- Lamač Miroslav: *Georges Braque*, Odeon, Prague, 1983
- Lukeš Zdeněk: *Praha moderní* [Modern Prague], Paseka, Prague, 2012
- Lukeš Zdeněk: *Český architektonický kubismus* [Czech Architectural Cubism], Galerie Jaroslava Fragnera: Dan Merta, Prague, 2006
- Lukeš Zdeněk: *Stavby a architekti pohledem Zdeňka Lukeše* [Buildings and Architects through the Eyes of Zdeněk Lukeš], Lidové noviny, Prague, 2012

- *Okkultismus und Avantgarde: von Munch bis Mondrian 1900—1915*, Edition Tertium, Ostfildern, 1995
- Roeová Sue: *Impresionisté — Jejich životní příběhy* [Impressionists — Their Life Stories], Metafora, Prague, 2012
- Rybár Ctibor: *Ulice a domy města Prahy* [The Streets and Buildings of the City of Prague], Victoria Publishing, Prague, 1996
- Scheufler Pavel: *Praha 1848—1914* [Prague of 1848—1914], Panorama, Prague, 1984
- Steiner Rudolf: *Die Alchemie des Alltags*, catalog, Vitra Design Museum, Weil am Rhein, 2011
- *Steiner Rudolf a současné umění* [Rudolf Steiner and Contemporary Art], catalog, DOX Centre for Contemporary Art, Prague, 2011
- *Steiner und die Kunst der Gegenwart*, catalog, Kunstmuseum Wolfsburg, Kunstmuseum Stuttgart, 2011
- *Sprechender Beton*, Verlag am Goetheanum, Dornach,1972
- Various authors: *Český kubismus 1909—1925* [Czech Cubism of 1909—1925], i3 CZ, Modernista, 2006
- Various authors: *Josef Gočár*, Titanic, Praha, 2010
- Various authors: *Umělecké památky Prahy — Nové Město a Vyšehrad, Staré Město a Josefov, Malá Strana, Hradčany a Pražský hrad* [Artistic Monuments of Prague — New Town and Vyšehrad; Old Town and Josefov; Lessor Town, Hradčany and the Prague Castle], Academia, Prague, 1998
- Vegesack Alexander von: *Tschechische Kubismus Architektur und Design 1910—1925*, Vitra Design Museum, Weil am Rhein, 1991
- Vlček Tomáš: *Praha 1900* [Prague of 1900], Panorama, Prague, 1986
- Wirth Zdeněk: *Staletá Praha* [Hundreds of Years of Prague], Jan Otto, Prague, 1942

ALPHABETICAL INDEX

P

ESOTERIC PRAGUE

CUBIST PRAGUE

Jan Boněk

English translation Zuzana Dussel Jurgens
Visual materials Petr Boněk, Jiří Kuchař, Tomáš Boněk
and archives of Pavel Scheufler and the publishing house

Cover design, layout & typography Adam Friedrich
Printed by Finidr, s. r. o., Český Těšín

Published by Eminent Publishing House
P. O. Box 298, CZ-11121 Prague 1, Czech Republic, EU
www.eminent-books.eu

14/01/30
ISBN 978–80–7281–469–5